4·21·04

362.829
Nel   Nelson, Noelle C.

        Dangerous rela-
        tionships

DUE DATE

Dangerous Relationships

How to Identify and Respond to the
Seven Warning Signs of a Troubled Relationship

Dangerous
Relationships

How to Identify and Respond to the
Seven Warning Signs of a Troubled Relationship

Noelle Nelson

PERSEUS PUBLISHING
Cambridge, Massachusetts

Many of the designations used by manufacturers and sellers to distinguish their products are claimed as trademarks. Where those designations appear in this book and Perseus Publishing was aware of a trademark claim, the designations have been printed in initial capital letters.

The relationships used as illustrations in this book are composites of individual cases. They represent the most common relationships involving domestic violence, as represented in the literature, and from my direct experience over the years as a practicing psychotherapist, clinical psychotherapist, and trial consultant. Names and many details have been changed to protect client confidentiality.

This book is not meant to replace ongoing support groups, therapy, or any other counseling. If you're getting help, keep it up! You're on the road to health and wholeness.

Copyright © 1997 by Noelle Nelson

Cataloging-in-Publication Data is available from the Library of Congress.
ISBN 0–7382-0465-X

Perseus Publishing is a member of the Perseus Books Group.
Find us on the World Wide Web at http://www.perseuspublishing.com

Perseus Publishing books are available at special discounts for bulk purchases in the U.S. by corporations, institutions, and other organizations. For more information, please contact the Special Markets Department at the Perseus Books Group, 11 Cambridge Center, Cambridge, MA 02142, or call (617)252-5298.

First paperback printing, March 2001
    3 4 5 6 7 8 9 10—03 02

Foreword

I have known Dr. Noelle Nelson's work as a clinician since 1987 and have been continuously impressed with her insight and skill as a clinical psychologist. She has used her years of experience in her work as a basis for *Dangerous Relationships*. Dr. Nelson reveals her personal journey as a clinician and shares many others' stories— their abuse, their pain, and their road to self-discovery. She offers examples of clients and their struggles and triumphs.

Dangerous Relationships is a must for any individual entering a relationship with doubt. Dr. Nelson has clearly developed guidelines that delineate the warning signs of abusive relationships. The book illustrates what kinds of relationships are dysfunctional from the outset and which ones are likely to succeed.

Dr. Nelson's characterization of the abuser is illu-minating. It becomes apparent as relationships progress that abusers follow a pattern in developing relationships.

As we increase our understanding of these patterns, we are better prepared to pursue healthy relationships. We can heal and grow with the knowledge and understanding that we have a choice to create a more positive, supportive, and healthier life. Dr. Nelson provides us with the awareness and tools to make more informed and, ultimately, wiser choices in our search for love and intimacy.

Dr. Nelson has done a brilliant job in identifying those behaviors that lead to abusive relationships. We are, indeed, indebted to Dr. Nelson for the insight and gentle guidance that she offers in this book. In a world where creating relationships is fraught with many perils and difficulties, Dr. Nelson has provided a valuable road map.

Marcia G. Lamm, Ph.D., Q.M.E.
Director, West Valley Psychological Clinic
Encino, California

Preface

Domestic violence hurts. It rips at the very fabric of what is most precious to us—our relationships with the ones we love. Domestic violence hurts not only those who are violated, but also the families of those involved and our society as a whole. As a clinical psychologist, therapist, and trial consultant, I have met and worked with too many individuals who have suffered from domestic violence. I was trained to sit quietly and listen to my clients with objectivity and a certain distancing, so as to better work with them in their search for health and wholeness. I found, however, that I could not sit quietly through tales of domestic violence! It was too painful, and I cared too much. I wanted to do more than just help those individuals who came to me for healing once the damage had already been done.

As I heard story after story of pain and heartache I realized that there were many similarities in these stories, even though the individuals involved were very different. This led me to research extensively the phenomenon of domestic violence. I discovered that there are certain key defining characteristics inherent to the very nature of these relationships—characteristics that appear in non-violent forms early on, usually within the first three months of the relationship. I knew that if I could sufficiently identify those characteristics and make them easily recognizable, they could serve as warning signs. These warning signs might enable people to spot potentially violent relationships before they become violent.

Domestic violence doesn't happen in a vacuum. Domestic violence is committed by a certain type of individual and occurs within a certain type of relationship. Abusive individuals are, at first, often very charming, taking care to present the side of themselves they know is most alluring. Their potential for violence can be easily missed. However, if one looks at the nature of the relationship, at the interplay between the partners, the warning signs of domestic violence, even during the first few months, are clear and virtually unmistakable.

This book does not address individuals who are currently experiencing a violent domestic relationship, for they are long past the beginning stages. Nor is it addressed to people who are not in a position of choice, such as children or the elderly living in an abusive household. This book is designed specifically to help individuals who are looking for love, romantic or platonic, to recognize the warning signs of a relationship that will nurture not love, but abuse.

There are two ways to end domestic violence. One way is to heal the domestic violence that is already going on in homes all over the country. The other way is to learn how to prevent domestic violence from happening in the first place. This book focuses on prevention: helping yourself and those you love recognize and respond appropriately to the warning signs of a potentially violent relationship.

Acknowledgments

I am deeply grateful to all those who had the courage to tell me their stories and thus give me the opportunity to contribute to the healing of domestic violence. I am also greatly appreciative of the constant support, encouragement, and valuable input from my colleagues, in particular Dr. Marcia Lamm, whose wisdom and friendship has guided me unerringly through the years. Special thanks to my editor, Frank K. Darmstadt, and his colleague, Charlie Cates, who saw the potential of the book when it was but a thin manuscript and wholeheartedly engaged in the vigorous dialogue that led to a solid work. As always, I thank Diane Rumbaugh for her marvelous ability to work with me and smile through it all and my friends and family, who put up with me when I'm in

"Don't talk to me, I'm writing" mode and are still there loving me when I resurface.

This book is dedicated to all those who have suffered the horrors of domestic violence. May your next relationship be the loving one you truly deserve.

Contents

Warning Sign #1: A Whirlwind Beginning

Warning Sign #2: Possessiveness

Warning Sign #4: Blame

Warning Sign #5: Verbal Abuse

Warning Sign #6: Insensitivity

Dangerous Relationships

How to Identify and Respond to the
Seven Warning Signs of a Troubled Relationship

Introduction

"I never believed it could happen to me!"

How often have I heard that cry as I have counseled yet another woman, sobbing as she tells me of how her boyfriend or husband beat her up, or yet another man, telling me of his lover's cruelty. People never believe domestic violence can happen to them. You don't fall in love with the expectation that you're headed for the emergency room, yet unless you know what to look for in a relationship, there is a chance that it is exactly where you are headed.

- ✓ The incidence of domestic violence is estimated at 4 million cases annually, or one assault every 15 seconds[1]
- ✓ Over 50 percent of all women murdered are killed by male partners, and 12 percent of murdered men are killed by female partners[2]

You are at risk! Given the statistics, it is critical for anyone seeking a relationship to learn about domestic violence and how to prevent it.

WHAT IS DOMESTIC VIOLENCE?

Domestic violence is a relatively neutral-sounding phrase that covers some not very neutral behavior: being hit, having things thrown at you, being pushed around, or otherwise being brutalized by those you are either living with or related to. Most often, domestic violence means being beaten up by those you love.

Domestic violence can happen to anyone at any time. Domestic violence does not respect age, gender, or sexual preference. Parents have hit their children, children have beaten up their parents, wives have knifed husbands, husbands have battered wives, brothers have hacked away at sisters, sisters have thrown countless objects at brothers. Cousins, uncles, aunts, live-in mates, girlfriends, boyfriends—all have been party to or victims of domestic violence.

This book is addressed to those who want to be in a healthy, happy, loving relationship, as lovers, partners, or friends, and who fear that they might be on the receiving end of violence. In a world of increasing violence and fear, it is important to be able to discern who is and who is not likely to hurt you. Such knowledge is far preferable to the alternatives—avoiding relationships entirely to be sure you won't get hurt or trusting to luck that somehow you won't get battered.

This book can also be of service to clinicians, to help assess whether clients are at risk of domestic violence.

Dangerous Relationships is not addressed to batterers or people who fear they might become violent in a relationship. The dynamics of those who perpetrate domestic violence are worthy of a separate book and are beyond the scope of this work.

THE PURPOSE OF THIS BOOK

If someone screamed at you or hit you the first time you met him or her, you'd know exactly what to do. You'd know that person meant trouble, and you'd want no part of it. The problem with a violent domestic relationship is that it doesn't start that way. Most relationships that end up in domestic violence start off as any nonviolent relationship does—with kind words and passion, togetherness and devotion. It may seem impossible to know the difference between the violent and the nonviolent until it's too late. Fortunately, that's not so.

A violent domestic relationship is a type of relationship that fosters the development and occurrence of abuse, most commonly in the form of battering. The violence that erupts comes out of a larger pattern of abusive behaviors, such as indifference to your needs, blaming you for everything that goes wrong, and being extremely possessive, which, although present in the relationship from its inception, are not usually recognized as abusive behaviors.

These behaviors, however, are readily identifiable and can be used as early indicators of possible future violence, long before you suffer from blows. The purpose of this book is to help you spot and then deal successfully with the seven key warning signs of a potentially violent domestic relationship. It will teach you what to look for and what to do so you don't end up on the receiving end of a loved one's fist.

The warning signs described in the following chapters are just that, warning signs. They are meant to alert you to the presence of possible danger ahead, much like a warning label on a bottle of medicine warns you of possible side effects. A warning label on a medicine bottle doesn't mean you will suffer the side effects, just as the presence of a warning sign in a relationship doesn't mean it will develop into a violent domestic relationship. However, a warning does mean you should pay attention. The more warning signs present in the relationship, the more aware you should be to the possibility that you are at risk. The more intense the warning signs, even if they are few, the more alert you must become.

Does that mean if you notice someone you're getting involved with is behaving according to one of the warning signs you should get out of the relationship? Not necessarily. What it means is that you need to pay attention to the warning sign and deal with it. People do, for example, blame others, without such behavior being indicative of a violent domestic relationship. Being aware of blaming as a warning sign gives you an opportunity to deal with your lover's/friend's blaming behavior. If you are successful in communicating with your partner the impact of always blaming you, you can work together to find healthier ways of sharing responsibility (see Chapter 10). You will be less likely to be involved in a violent domestic relationship. If, however, you cannot, and your lover/friend continues to blame you for anything and everything, you may very well be in the beginning stages of a violent domestic relationship and should start thinking seriously about whether you want to stay in that relationship.

Because this book approaches domestic violence prevention from a real-life problem-solving perspective, it shows you the warning signs in real relationships: Mary/John (heterosexual lovers), Bob/Karen (husband and wife), Peter/Tony (homosexual lovers), Teri/Anne (platonic roommates). Since no two relationships are alike, you may find aspects of each of the four illustrative relationships that apply to you. Whatever your gender, age, and sexual preference, read through *all* of the examples, and then go back and focus on the situation that seems closest to your own.

As different as these four relationships may appear on the surface, they have very similar underlying dynamics. Each of the relationships has an active partner, the abuser who perpetrates the violence, and a passive partner, the person who is violated. The active partner is the more obvious, since he or she is the one doing the kicking and screaming. However, long before the active partner becomes overtly violent, he or she has behaved abusively toward the passive partner. Because these early abusive behaviors are subtle, the passive partner generally does not recognize them for what they are: preludes to violence.

Dangerous Relationships is written from the perspective of the passive partner. The passive partners, Mary, Bob, Peter, and Teri, did not recognize the potential for danger in their relationships. How could they? We are not taught "The Anatomy of a Violent Domestic Relationship" in school. We are largely unaware of how a relationship in which violence is possible develops. We are thus unable to respond in a healthy and successful manner to the beginnings of such a relationship. No wonder passive partners often feel so helpless and hopeless in the face of domestic violence! Yet as abusers, John, Karen, Tony, and Anne all behaved in certain characteristic predictable ways, which almost inevitably lead to violence in a domestic relationship. The predictability of an abuser's behavior is what makes domestic violence, to a large degree, preventable. Because it is difficult, if not often impossible, to stop the violence once it starts, learning to identify the warning signs of a potentially violent domestic relationship and how to deal with the situation appropriately and immediately can significantly contribute to your future health and well-being in relationships.

CAUTION

There are no guarantees in relationships. Although the great majority of violent domestic relationships are preceded by the warning signs described in this book, some violence does come "out of the blue." Use this book as you would a manual for safe driving: You can't prevent all accidents from happening, but safe driving habits will certainly minimize your chances of getting into an accident. Similarly, you can't predict all occurrences of domestic violence, but safe relationship habits will certainly diminish the likelihood of your finding yourself in a potentially violent relationship.

If you are currently experiencing domestic violence—beating, shoving, hitting, or any other violation of your human rights—*call your local domestic violence hotline immediately*. In the "Resources" chapter of this book you will find a listing of a number of organizations that can help you with more detailed information. The "Personalized Safety Plan" has also been included to give you ideas on how to help yourself.

HOW TO USE THIS BOOK

The first seven parts of the book discuss the seven key warning signs of a potentially violent domestic relationship. Each section contains chapters detailing the warning signs, breaking them down into easily recognizable parts, with examples from the four relationships to illustrate how the warning signs show up differently in different relationships. The companion chapters to each warning sign focus on how to respond to the behavior, that is, what to do when you encounter one of the signs in a relationship.

The first section deals with the passionate beginning of a violent domestic relationship and how to differentiate between healthy intensity and dangerous intensity.

The second section looks at possessiveness, the kind that is normal in a relationship and the kind that seeks to control and dominate you.

The third section introduces you to the quick and sudden personality changes abusers make, from Mr./Ms. Wonderful into a monster you wish you had never met.

The fourth section alerts you to the abuser's blaming behavior, where you are wrong about everything, while the abuser is always right.

The fifth section discusses verbal abuse, words that criticize, demean, and cut you to the quick.

The sixth section examines the insensitive attitude abusers have toward the fate of others, an indifference that sets the stage for violence.

The seventh section exposes how the violence is too often minimized and made acceptable, denied and pushed away, only to have it come back worse.

The last section revisits Mary, Bob, Peter, and Teri and lets you know how each of them used the skills and awarenesses they learned to help them move forward with their lives.

NOTES

1. Richard Jones III, "Let Our Voices Be Heard: Domestic Violence," *Obstetrics and Gynecology*, *81*(1), January 1993.
2. Susan McLeer *et al.* "The Role of the Emergency Physician in the Prevention of Domestic Violence," *Annals of Emergency Medicine*, *16*(10), October 1987.

The Four Relationships

The relationships that we focus on in this book ended up as follows:

Mary, a 45-year-old cashier at the local grocery mart, was beaten to the point of unconsciousness by her lover of two years, John, because she was late coming home from work. It was the fourth such beating that year.

Bob, a 52-year-old engineer, was diagnosed with an ulcer, panic attacks, and clinical depression when his romantic fling with a co-worker, Karen, turned into a nightmarish marriage where insults and objects were hurled at him in equal measure.

Peter, a 31-year-old production assistant, lay in a hospital bed seriously injured after his lover of six months, Tony, tried to strangle him for supposed infidelity. Peter was found by the apartment super who was concerned by his apparent absence two days after Tony had left him for dead.

Teri, a 24-year-old insurance clerk, came home one night horrified to find that her roommate, Anne, had torched all her belongings, set in a near pile in the middle of the living room of the apartment they shared. Anne was enraged with Teri for never spending time with her anymore. The fire department managed to put the fire out before the entire building was engulfed. It was only as the firefighters were sorting through the debris that Teri realized Anne had also torched her cat.

Tragic stories. Damaged lives, all derailed by domestic violence.

But that's not where these relationships began. Instead, they began, as all love stories do, with happiness and sweet words, hearts and flowers.

A Whirlwind Beginning

ONE

Swept Away

ISN'T IT ROMANTIC

"Tell me how it all began," I said. The attractive middle-aged woman in front of me sighed, looked out my office window for a moment, then said, "How it all began? It seems so long ago—like on some other planet!" I waited patiently. It had taken Mary much courage to start therapy. She'd only left her abusive relationship three weeks ago and her wounds, emotional as well as physical, were still fresh. Finally Mary spoke up again: "How it all started? With a kiss! Literally, with a kiss."

Now that she'd started, Mary found it easier to go on. "I was running an errand for our store manager, delivering receipt envelopes to the accounting offices, and as I was rushing down the hall, I heard someone yell 'Wait.' I turned around and there was this great looking guy—real handsome, rugged, kind of like the Marlboro man—and he was holding one of the envelopes I'd apparently dropped. 'You dropped this,' he said, coming over to give it back to me. I put my hand out to take it, and before I could do that he took my hand and kissed it—real nice—and said, 'You're so beautiful,' and then he like blushed and stammered and dropped my hand real quick and said, 'I shouldn't have done that, I shouldn't have said that, I'm sorry, I'm sorry,' and he's backing away and I said 'No, it's OK—it is—thanks for picking up my envelope,' and he said, 'Really, you're not upset with me?' and I said, 'No, thanks,' and I turned to go. I mean I was getting later by the minute and he said, 'Can I call you? What's your name?'and I'm running at this point, I'm late, and I yelled out, 'Sure! It's Mary—I'm at the Grocery Mart on 3rd Street,' and kept running. He flashed this great grin at me and just stood there looking until I disappeared out the door.

"When I walked into the store the next morning, there was a single red rose at my checkstand, with a card that just said 'Delivered with a kiss' on it. No name. But I knew exactly who it was. And then he called. And that's how it all got started."

Mary looked at me for a moment, "Sounds incredible, doesn't it? But that's just how it was—incredible. Like something out of a romance novel." Mary continued her story: "I was in heaven. I've never felt so beautiful, so wanted, so loved. This was a fairy tale come true—the most marvelously romantic relationship I'd ever had! John was wonderfully passionate, intense, right from the beginning. I mean, on our third date, he told me I was the woman he'd always dreamed of, that I made him forget all the others. He'd bring me a rose, a single red rose, every time we had a date. After the first week, well, we pretty much were together all the time. I went to bed with him on the second date. I know that was kind of quick, but he was so ardent, he wanted me so badly, I guess he kind of bowled me over."

ADAM AND EVE IN PARADISE

"How it all began?" Bob shook his head. "From the way it all began, Doc, I never would have guessed this ending." Bob had divorced his second wife of just 18 months, Karen, less than half a year ago, a wrenching parting that still tugged and pulled at his heart, even though he knew that it was the only sane thing to do. "The beginning was paradise," Bob said, "Hokey as it sounds, that's what it was—Adam and Eve in paradise."

"I've never been so loved by a woman," Bob continued. "Never. She couldn't keep her hands off me. It was great. Karen had this slinky way with her eyes, she was always looking at me, like eating me up with her eyes. And she was so exciting—right from the start. She wanted to be with me and do it all the time, telling me how I was the best. She couldn't get enough of me, how I turned her on like no other man.

"From another woman, wanting to be with me all the time like that, I would have felt suffocated—but Karen was different—she wasn't clingy, wanting me to be sappy and calling her all the time. She was exciting. She never called to say 'I miss you, where are you?' Karen would call and first thing out of her mouth would be 'I can feel your hands all over me, making me wet—I can feel them so much it's like you were here right now, oh, I can't take it—' and she'd moan and hang up. I'd be standing there like an idiot, listening to a dial tone, erect as all get out. I couldn't get over to her place fast enough. And it was all the time like that. It's almost like she didn't care what I did, whatever I did, it was great, it excited her. Man, she was a trip!"

Bob got up and paced as he continued, memories returning quickly now. "Even the way we met was exciting. I'd been transferred to another department and so I was just meeting everybody for the first time. People were being real nice, making an effort to introduce them-selves, and like that. Karen waltzed into my office with a big cup of hot coffee, sat it on the desk in front of me, perched herself on the side of the desk, crossing those unbelievable legs of hers in this short skirt, and said in a real seductive voice, 'Nice and hot, just like you like it—I hope.' I was stunned. No one had ever come on to me like that—but before I had a chance to react, the woman laughed, hopped off the desk and stuck out her hand at me, 'Hi, I'm Karen. Welcome to the department. We're gonna get along just fine.' She winked and she was out that door. Man. I didn't know what hit me! Talk about outrageous flirt! No one ever flirted with me like that. I'm an ordinary guy, just your regular Joe, I'm OK, but come on, I'm no looker! Well, that didn't matter to Karen, she flirted with me so hard you'd have had to be a monk to resist her.

"I fell all right, hard. By the end of the first week she started in on me, I couldn't live without her." The sadness welled up in Bob's voice as he said, "Didn't want to."

A LOVE FOR ALL ETERNITY

"Funny you should ask that," said Peter, a pleasant-looking man with a somewhat quizzical expression, of my "Tell me how it all began" opener. "I've been going over the beginning in my mind a lot lately. Of course," he grimaced, lightly touching the side of his neck that was still bruised from his ex-lover Tony's attack several weeks back, "I've had a lot of time to think about these things." "I'm sure you have," I said quietly. "What sticks out most in your mind about how it all began?" Peter thought for a moment, then asked, "How much do you know about the gay community?" "A fair amount," I answered. "I have a number of gay clients."

Peter nodded "Well, sex often happens quickly in the gay community. It just seems to be one of those things. So I wasn't surprised when Tony wanted to sleep with me right away. But what got to me, I mean really got to me, was how romantic he was! We'd met at a gay club, had sex that night, he left, and I thought, great, that was nice. But the next day, he called first thing in the morning, just to tell me he was thinking of me and how wonderful I was and what a terrific lover I was and wanted to see me again right away.

"I thought it was just a sex thing, but when I left work, I found this silly sweet romantic card on the windshield of my car. When I met him later at the club, he had eyes only for me. We didn't sleep together that night—he said he wanted to cherish just being near me."

Peter was quiet for a moment, lost in his memories. Then, stirring himself, he said, "I started to think, maybe this wasn't just a sex thing, and the next day, you know what he did the next day? He had balloons delivered to my work. He showed up at my door that night with this terrific dinner packed in a picnic basket, which he proceeded to unload in the middle of my living room floor, all because I'd mentioned to him when we were talking the night before how I loved picnics.

"Tony made love to me by candlelight and told me I was the best thing that ever happened to him, that he could think of nothing more wonderful than lying in each other's arms for all eternity. Heck, I was hooked."

A DYNAMITE ROOMMATE

The young woman sat awkwardly on my couch, twisting her hands nervously in front of her. "I don't know what I'm doing here," she said. "There's nothing you can do, I mean—it's over." I nodded, waiting. "It's just that I can't sleep, I keep dreaming about the fire. And I'm so scared of people now. I don't understand why it happened. Nothing seems to make sense to me anymore." "Well," I said gently, "maybe if you talk about it, I can help you sort some of it out. Maybe together we can make some sense of it." "Maybe," Teri said, without much hope in her voice. "Why don't you start at the beginning?" I said. "Tell me how you first met Anne, how you became roommates."

"Well, let's see," Teri said. "I moved to the city from the small town I'd grown up in, and right away I started working for X & Y Company. I didn't know much of anything about the insurance business. I was a real raw recruit. I was fumbling, having trouble with stuff, and along came Anne. She was like a savior to me! She'd already been with the company a year or so, and she took it upon herself to show me the ropes. And that was great. She was always willing to help me out, seemed she always had time for me. Right away we started going to lunch together and walking to the parking lot together after work, and she'd call and we'd chat after hours. I didn't know anyone yet, having just moved in and all, so I was happy to have found a friend so quickly." Teri blushed, averting her eyes momentarily. "At first I thought maybe Anne had a 'thing' for me, you know? I mean, I'm naive, but I'm not *that* naive.... Anyway, I found out she had boyfriends from time to time, and she never touched me or talked to me in that way, so hey, I relaxed."

"Anne was really nice," Teri continued. "She'd get free tickets to go to ball games and the movies, and we had a great time. She was always telling me how smart I was and how funny, and how much more interesting I was than all the other girls at work. I couldn't see it myself, heck, she was the one who was smart and funny— and real pretty to boot. I was surprised she didn't have other friends she wanted to spend time with, but she said most people were boring, except for me, of course, and at the time, I wasn't interested in pursuing the issue. All I know is, she made me feel great.

"Anne suggested, about three weeks after I met her, that we should look for an apartment to room together. I would have loved to, but I told Anne I couldn't, I'd signed a six-month lease. Anne said that was no problem, and you know what? Two days later, she pranced into my cubicle with a cat-got-the-cream grin on her face and slapped a piece of paper down on my desk showing that I was released from the lease! I was amazed—she just laughed and said, 'I usually get what I want.' Then she said, 'Better start packing'—and she was out that door laughing the whole way down the hall. I thought, wow! This is great! Here's someone I like, who treats me terrific, and who would make a dynamite roommate. So we did it. She found a place and we moved in together the next week." Teri stopped in her recitation: "And that's how I met Anne, how we became roommates. If I'd only known what she was really like, I'd never have done it," she said wistfully. "If I'd only known."

Case Analysis

Whether romantic, sexual, or platonic, the beginning of a violent domestic relationship is typically intense. It has an exciting, impassioned quality that tends to unsettle people, throw them off their usual emotional moorings. This puts you at risk, for there are already patterns of abusive behavior evident that you might not notice given the initial excitement of the relationship. The purpose of this chapter is to describe the abusive characteristics as they first appear in a relationship so you can easily recognize them as early warning signs of potential domestic violence.

TOO MUCH, TOO SOON

You are getting everything you ever wanted in a relationship—so much attention, romantic and otherwise, so much affection, and so many compliments that you're carried along on a veritable sea of wonderful emotions and it all feels so good. You never want it to end.

So what's the problem? You're getting too much, too soon. The problem is that all those flattering words, all that attention and affection, are acting like a drug. The brain has a "pleasure center," which when stimulated produces endorphins, the neurotransmitters that make you feel good. When people are flooded with so much of what "feels good," nothing else matters. It's as if the individual's ability to think rationally is put on hold. In scientific experiments, rats that are given cocaine when they press on a bar will literally press that bar until they die. They cease to eat, drink, or do anything else that is "normal." So too do humans. When given their drug of choice over and over and over they seemingly lose the ability to think straight.

The person being showered with attention and affection doesn't look at the giver of such delights with any degree of objectivity. He or she wants to believe that it's for real. The individual's normal ability to evaluate and form opinions gets put on hold as he or she gives in to the pleasurable feelings of the moment. They are "hooked" on the good feelings just as an addict is hooked on drugs. There is little if any thought given to future consequences or implications.

The Drug of Romance

Romance can be a particularly potent drug. John made one romantic gesture after another in such rapid sequence that Mary was emotionally overwhelmed. We forget that it is just as possible to be emotionally overwhelmed with positive feelings as it is to be overwhelmed with negative ones, and just as mind-numbing. John flooded Mary with romance—kissing her hand, staring longingly after her, delivering a single red rose with no name on the card (the adoring mystery man, an undying romantic fantasy), then giving her a red rose on every date. Mary rapidly became hooked on the romance. In this condition, she was unable to stop and look at John to see who he really was, she could only see him as the dispenser of romantic "goodies."

Hooked on Sexual Desirability

Bob got "hooked" on how sexually attractive and desirable Karen's overt sexual advances made him feel. Although Bob wasn't particularly insecure in the sexual arena, he'd never received the kind or amount of sexual attention Karen gave him. Had Karen made her advances within the context and steady progression of a relationship, Bob would not have been emotionally overwhelmed. But in the face of such consistent, persistent sexual attention from a desirable woman, Bob felt unbelievably sexually desirable for the first time in his life. That is a tremendously powerful drug.

Not only were Karen's advances way beyond anything Bob had ever experienced before, but she made her advances immediately, before Bob had any way of integrating Karen's sexual behavior into the overall nature of the relationship. This exemplifies the "too soon" aspect of a violent domestic relationship particularly well.

A Matter of Timing

It isn't just the *amount* of attention and affection that sends people into an emotional tailspin, but also the *timing* involved. In other words, if your partner becomes more romantic or sexually attracted to you over the years of your relationship, you have a way of integrating the increased attention and affection within the context of the whole of the relationship. You are able to take it "in stride." When such attention or affection comes all at once at the beginning of the relationship, there is no way to put such behavior in context. There isn't enough experience of the other to formulate a realistic assessment of what his or her behavior means. Yet the human mind seeks to attach significance to what happens to us, so people will quickly assign meaning to their lover's or friend's behavior largely determined by their feeling at that moment. Under these conditions it is difficult, if not impossible to attribute realistic or appropriate significance to the behavior.

This is very much like what happens to prisoners who have been brainwashed. They are deluged with so much information under high-stress conditions that they are unable to process the information appropriately and put it in a realistic or appropriate context. They literally can't think straight. Nor can you, in the presence of too much affection and attention too soon.

The Drug of Specialness

In Peter and Tony's relationship, the "too much, too soon" was the feeling Peter got of being so special that someone would pay attention to his smallest desire (picnics), so special that he made another's total happiness. This is probably one of the most seductive of all attention and affection drugs. It feels great to be special to someone, to be told that you make someone feel so terrific that he or she cherishes just being near you—that's powerful stuff! It's very hard to keep your rational mind in the driver's seat when you're being flooded with such statements. Also, Tony was backing up those statements with exquisite attention to what Peter liked—picnics and candlelight.

When a person pays attention to what you like and want, it is natural to think that you have meaning for that person, you are important to that person. In many cases that is true, but when individuals pay too much attention to *your* wants and needs too soon in a relationship, they are frequently not revealing who they are, with *their* wants and needs. It is difficult to see who the person is behind the wonderfully satisfying feeling of getting what you enjoy. Therefore, decisions are made about individuals not based on who those individuals are, but on the good feelings you're getting from their attention. Once again, decisions are being made under the influence of an emotional drug.

Attention Is Addictive

Teri found herself hooked on attention, large doses of attention and lots of compliments. Within the first week of their meeting on the job, Anne was behaving toward Teri as a long-time best friend— having lunch together, walking out to the parking lot together, chatting after work every night, taking Teri to movies and ballparks, telling Teri how terrific she was. Overwhelmed by the pleasure of such attention, Teri didn't look at the unreality of the relationship: Anne really didn't know Teri at all.

Teri certainly didn't know Anne any better. You can't know someone in a week to the degree that a best friend does over a period of years. You can be fascinated by someone in a very short space of time, but you really don't *know* that person. Yet, flooded as she was by the very powerful good feelings engendered by Anne's attention, Teri didn't stop to think about the nature of the person with whom she might actually be getting involved. She just rode the "feel goods" and based her decision to become roommates on those feelings alone.

Drugs interfere with people's thinking process. Drugs interfere with good judgment. When people are on drugs, they don't make good decisions because they are not able to see things the way they really are. Too much attention or affection given too soon, be that romantic, sexual, or platonic, affects people just as drugs do. This overwhelming attention interferes with the ability to see things the way they really are, to think clearly. It impedes judgment and the ability to make good decisions for oneself.

THE PUSH FOR INTIMACY

There you are, riding high on a sea of wonderful emotions, and your new lover or friend pressures you to do something that's uncomfortable for you, for example, wants to have sex before you're really ready, or wants to see you more than you'd really like, or wants to move in together right away. Flooded overall with good feelings, you override your discomfort and go along with your partner's desire. You dismiss your feeling of being bulldozed into doing something you didn't really want to do. You ignore the long-term implications of overriding what's right for you in order to please your friend.

People who can easily and appropriately ask others for what they want or need don't have to bulldoze or manipulate. Abusers aren't good at asking for what they need. Abusers are often so out of touch with their emotions that they don't even know what they want; they just feel intense urges or internal pushes they need to satisfy immediately. Once a relationship has developed to the point of violence, these urges often take the form of "see red" or "get mad." At the beginning of such a relationship, however, such urges are expressed as having to be with you all time or having to be sexually intimate. These expressions can be very appealing, and their demanding quality is all too often overlooked.

The Push for Sexual Intimacy

Certainly Mary found John's push for intimacy appealing. How could she deny such a passionate intense suitor his desire to be with her all the time, his desire for sexual fulfillment? After all, wasn't John doing all the "right" romantic things—roses, kisses, passionate statements? In talking with Mary later, she disclosed that she was uncomfortable with giving John so much of her time so soon, and most definitely would have preferred that they wait a while longer before sleeping together. She felt, however, a sense of the inevitable, or, as Mary puts it, "Well, it was going to come to this, we were going to be together and of course we were going to make love, so I felt kind of stupid saying no." Given her state of emotional overwhelm, Mary wasn't thinking well, wasn't processing the information she really needed to look at, and was all too easy for John to convince. She assumed, as most of us do, that physical intimacy, both time spent together and sexual intimacy, meant that intimacy of the heart—the tenderness—would be there as well.

True intimacy is born out of closeness and familiarity with a person. To be intimate with someone means to know their ins and outs, to be familiar with all parts of them, and to be tender toward all those different aspects. You may not like your best friend's every decision and behavior, but if you are genuinely intimate with your friend, you will have a compassion and tenderness toward him or her that you would not necessarily have toward another person making the same decision or exhibiting the same behavior. Abusers feel within themselves a tremendous push to get close to the other person very quickly. They will seek shortcuts to that closeness, in the form of moving in together or having sex, for example. The problem is, while you think closeness implies the tenderness and compassion that go along with genuine intimacy, to abusers, closeness in and of itself is intimacy. Abusers, lacking an emotional connection to themselves, are unable for the most part to connect in tender or compassionate ways with others. Closeness without tenderness is dangerous. Abusive parents are a prime example of how horrific close relationships can be in the absence of tenderness and compassion. Violent domestic relationships are another.

The Demand for Passionate Sexuality

In Bob's case, the push for intimacy took the form of passionate sexuality. Bob was only too happy to accede to Karen's demand to see him all the time, because every time he saw her, she wanted—and gave—plenty of very exciting sex. He didn't stop to think about what the implications were of her wanting to see him all the time, apart from the sexuality of their encounters. As exemplified in the movie *Fatal Attraction*, passionate sexuality may not be good for your health. Given the intensity of his emotional state, Bob wasn't asking himself what might be motivating Karen's passion, what it might mean in the larger scheme of things, or where it might lead. He certainly didn't realize the import of the message he was giving Karen by so eagerly responding to her every call: "I'm yours any way you want me anytime."

The Power of Intimate Words

Peter did not perceive Tony's desire to have sex the first night as a push for intimacy—far from it. Such episodes are, according to Peter, common in the gay community. Tony's push for intimacy took a different tack. Three days after their meeting, Tony told Peter he was the best thing that ever happened to him and that he could think of nothing more wonderful than lying in each other's arms for all eternity.

If you look at this statement objectively, it's impossible. Tony hardly knew Peter at all at this stage of the relationship. Saying that Peter was "the best thing" is completely unrealistic. Such a statement is an expression of Tony's inner push for closeness, not a statement of true intimacy. To Peter's ear, however, it sounded like an intimate statement, one that would carry with it all the tenderness and caring implicit in intimacy. Given the heady feelings of specialness Tony's attention had nurtured in Peter, Peter was susceptible to such a push for intimacy. He went along with Tony's "lying in each other's arms for all eternity" without thinking what that statement meant, or what the reality of a relationship with Tony meant. Peter acceded to Tony's push for intimacy, not realizing what he'd just said yes to.

The Push for Togetherness

Teri didn't give much thought to Anne's push for intimacy. Teri was enjoying how she felt around Anne and the fun of the relationship. She really didn't see the push until I pointed it out to her. "Didn't you think it was a little strange that Anne couldn't wait out the term of your lease for the two of you to move in together?" I asked Teri during the course of a session. "You know," Teri answered, "I was so blown away by how she did it — got me out of my lease, I didn't really think about it. But you're right. It doesn't make sense. I mean, we could be just as good friends living together as not, and it would have been something to look forward to." "Yes," I nodded, "but Anne couldn't wait." "No," Teri agreed wryly, "Anne always had to have her way, and she had to have it NOW!"

Anne's inner push, her need to get close fast, was hidden in how cleverly she'd gone about it. By going along with Anne's desire, Teri let Anne know she could be bulldozed. The fact that Teri never even noticed what was going on is typical of how the passive partner of a violent domestic relationship contributes to the development of the relationship—by not responding, thinking objectively, or taking the time to sort out the implications and consequences of the active partner's behavior.

HIGH UP ON A PEDESTAL

You're ecstatic, glowing with joy and love of life. Last night, on your third date, your new found significant other told you, "You're my reason for living, you're the sunshine in my life," and you've been walking on air ever since. How exciting, how wonderful to hear such thrilling words. However, at this stage of a relationship, such words have little foundation. If indeed after the third date you are someone's reason for living, then at the very least you should wonder what that person has been living for before meeting you. This person hardly knows you at this stage of the relationship, so what is it about you then that makes you his or her reason for living?

Their expectations of you. Once abusers have put a person on the pedestal of wonderfulness, have determined that this person is the one destined to be their reason for living, the light of their life, the partner they have always dreamed of, they expect that individual to live up to the description. It is the partner's inevitable failure to live up to such an unrealistic expectation that leads to much of the violence in these relationships.

The Woman of His Dreams

John put Mary on such a pedestal early in the relationship, saying she was the woman he had always dreamed of, long before he knew Mary well enough to determine that she was indeed that woman. Yet once he put Mary on that pedestal, John expected her to stay there, fulfilling all his expectations. In other words, Mary didn't exist in this relationship as an autonomous being. Mary existed in this relationship to fulfill John's wants and needs.

As long as Mary did fulfill John's wants and needs, Mary would be the love of his life. Should she fail to fulfill John's expectations at any time, she would fall from that pedestal of worship and adoration. Just by Mary being who she was, a fallible human being, Mary would at some time do or say something that failed to live up to John's preformed expectations, and that's when Mary would be at risk for violence.

What distinguishes abusers from other types of individuals is this expectation abusers have of their partners to live up to the *abusers'* definition of them, not to their *partners'* definition of themselves. A nonabusive person could say "You're the greatest" and mean simply that his partner is the most wonderful sexual partner he has thus far encountered. When an abuser makes such a statement, that abuser expects the other to be "the greatest" all the time from that moment on.

The Greatest Lover

Having declared Bob to be "the greatest" in bed, Karen expected Bob to fulfill all her sexual needs forevermore. This is an impossible sexual pedestal. What if Bob failed to bring Karen to orgasm one day? What if he was tired and didn't want to make love? What if he was depressed and couldn't make love? In other words, what if Bob behaved like the normal human being he was? Sooner or later he would, and that's when he would find himself in a potentially violent situation.

The Best Thing Ever

Tony put Peter on the pedestal called "best thing that ever happened to me" within the first three days of their meeting each other. Tony hardly knows Peter at this point, yet already Peter is dangerously set up to be that "best thing." The day Peter fails to live up to Tony's description, as he must, being human and likely to do or say something Tony will not judge is "best," is the day Tony will turn on him.

Never Boring

Anne, in a less direct yet equally emphatic way, created unrealistic expectations of Teri. Teri was perfectly happy to accept Anne's friendship. Why question a good thing? Teri didn't notice the unrealistic expectations that were building. For example, Anne said Teri was "never boring"; one day, inevitably, Teri would be—everybody is—and then what? What of Anne's expectation that Teri would always be available to accompany Anne wherever she wanted whenever she wanted and to talk on the telephone every night? Surely this availability would change as Teri came to know more people and make new friends. What then?

When people know each other over long periods of time and have had the opportunity to see the wonderful as well as the not-so-wonderful sides of each other, such a statement as "You are the love of my life" is no longer one of expectation, but an observation, genuinely felt, derived from shared experiences. It has emotional truth to it. As with many of the potential abuser's behaviors, it's not the behavior in and of itself that tells you trouble may lie ahead. It's the inappropriate intensity, exaggeration, or timing of the behavior that says "beware."

TWO

How to Deal with the Heady Rush
of a Passionate Beginning

TOO MUCH, TOO SOON

When you are in the midst of receiving an abundance of attention and affection from a person you are attracted to, the last thing you want to do is cry "Halt!" However, that's exactly what you need to do. Don't put a halt to the attention and affection, but give yourself some time to think.

Your ability to think things through is a precious and wonderful gift that, unfortunately, most of us throw out the window as soon as our emotions get going. The first thing to ask yourself is *"Is this a person I really want to get involved with?"* Just because he throws flowers, gifts, compliments, and soulful looks your way doesn't mean this is an appropriate individual for you to welcome into your life!

Just Having Fun

"Well it doesn't really matter who he is, I'm just having fun. I'm not looking for 'forever' lover," you say, "this is just for now." You may think you can just have fun and perhaps that is so. But what if the other person is serious about his or her attraction to you? What do you think might happen if a potentially violent individual realizes you are treating his or her feelings for you lightly? Toying with people's emotions is not wise, and even less so with violently inclined individuals. Whether you are interested in just having an affair or looking for a lifelong friendship and mate, do not give in to the emotion of the moment at the expense of your ability to think. Pay attention to who your partner is.

Who *Is* Your Partner?

Whirlwind beginnings usually last about three months. During that time, it is extremely important for you to repeatedly ask yourself, "What do I know about this individual? Does what I know about her fit with what I want for myself at this time in my life? Does what she wants in her life fit with what I want in mine?"

"Yes, but Dr. Noelle," you ask, "won't that spoil all the fun? Who wants to ask questions when you're in the middle of a romantic moment?" Who said you have to ask such questions in the middle of a romantic moment? There are plenty of quiet times between romantic moments to do so, and these are the very questions that may save you from becoming involved with a dangerous individual.

Ask Questions

Ask questions about your new lover's/friend's values, beliefs on such matters as how men and women should behave toward one another or what friends should be willing to do for each other. Ask about their hopes, dreams, fears, and worries. Find out what is great about their life and what is not so great. Get to know your new lover or friend: Ask about past relationships, hobbies, interests, friends, as many facets of that person's life as you can think of. Listen carefully to the answers. If your new love, for example, tells you that all the other relationships in his life didn't work out because the people he got involved with were all just out for themselves, think about that. Most people have upsides and downsides. When someone reports that all previous relationship partners only had downsides, that's a warning. What does such a comment say about your new love's choice of partners or how your new friend ends up justifying the inability to develop a healthy relationship, for example? What might that mean in the context of a relationship with you? Think about it.

"Geez," you say, "I don't want to have to analyze everything to death." You don't have to. Just be willing to think a little, enough to evaluate: "How realistic is what she is saying or doing? What does it tell me about her? What might it mean for me? Does this fit for me?"

Don't accept answers such as "Love is all that matters," "All I care about is you, nothing else counts," or "I think you're terrific, that's all that's important." As flattering as such answers may be, they don't tell you much about the person saying them. Appreciate the sentiment, but seek a more grounded answer. Get to know the person as an individual, including thoughts and feelings about life and other people quite independent of how she or he feels about you.

Slow Down

As thrilling as it may be to have someone want to be with you morning, noon and night, such intensity creates too heady an environment. Emotions reign to the detriment of clear thinking. You don't have to get swept away. You can take your time, *slow down*, and allow the relationship to develop at a pace that accommodates both thinking and feeling. Often this means setting limits for yourself, for example, resisting the temptation to talk for hours on the telephone every single day. If you've talked for two hours on one day on the telephone, allow a day or two to go by with just a brief call, or none at all. Don't see each other every day, all day and all night the first few weeks. Give yourself breathing room between encounters so the intensity of the emotions does not build up to such a degree that you are engulfed and can no longer think clearly.

Losing Interest

"But if I do that," you ask, "won't he lose interest?" Maybe. But then ask yourself, if this new love loses interest just because you aren't available to him 24 hours a day, every day, what does it say about the nature of his interest? Was he really ever interested in you at all? Or was he just interested in having an intense relationship, and you were a likely candidate?

This attitude is typical of abusers, so yes, they are likely to disappear if you don't fulfill their need for intensity. In that case, what have you lost?

Someone who is genuinely interested in you as a unique human being, however, is going to be willing to take the time to get to know you. She is not going to go anywhere just because you prefer to take it a little slow. Trust your value. Know that you are worth taking time to get to know. Be willing to risk that some individuals may not want to take that time. So be it—it's their loss. Be willing to wait until someone genuinely interested in you comes along.

THE PUSH FOR INTIMACY

Intimacy and sex are not synonymous. It is perfectly possible to have sex without being intimate. It is equally possible to be intimate without having sex. Intimacy implies tenderness toward and closeness with another person. When you are intimate with someone, you become vulnerable to that person. You are revealing all of you— the good parts, the not-so-good parts, and the downright nasty parts. You trust your partner to treat you and all the parts of you with caring and respect. Intimacy, therefore, is grounded in trust. Until trust has had an opportunity to develop, it is difficult to let go and be genuinely intimate with someone. Trust takes time to develop. It cannot be forced, just as you cannot force someone to be intimate with you, in the true definition of intimacy as tenderness and closeness.

"Making" Love Happen

When someone makes intimate gestures very early on, physically or verbally, he or she may be trying to force a close relationship into existence prematurely, before there is a genuine foundation for such intimacy. People generally try to force intimacy in order to create a bond, to "make" love happen as opposed to allowing love to happen. Abusive individuals, who have poor self-worth and low self-esteem, are afraid (on a subconscious level) that they are worthless. They fear that if you get a chance to know them, you'd probably see they are worthless and want to have nothing to do with them. Abusive individuals push intimacy in the hopes that you will fall in love with them, and that once you fall in love, you won't leave them even when you discover their worthlessness.

When It Feels Right

Most people have an inner sense of when it is "right" for them to accept intimate gestures. Too few of us, however, listen to that inner sense. We tend to talk ourselves into feeling the way the other person wants us to feel: "Maybe I'm being a prude," you say, to answer your discomfort with a sexual request. "I shouldn't be so old-fashioned; who waits these days?" "He says he loves me, I'd better say I love him too," you say to yourself, even though you're not sure about it yet. This kind of self-convincing is based on fear, fear that the other will leave, and with him, all the attention and affection goodies you've been getting. This kind of thinking puts you at risk: An individual who is unwilling to respect your timetable for intimacy is unlikely to respect your feelings in other matters.

Be True to Yourself

Listen to your feelings. When your "gut" tells you it is too soon for you to be intimate, verbally or physically, *it is too soon*. Believe it: Your gut is telling you that you do not yet feel safe with that person, you do not yet totally trust your partner to treat you and all the parts of you with respect and caring. Whether or not somewhere down the road you will feel safe and trusting of this individual is irrelevant; right now you don't. Honor yourself. Don't accept another's definition of when it's right for you to be intimate—only *you* know that.

Be true to your feelings of what does and doesn't feel comfortable. Don't get intimidated by the other's pressing need to be intimate. Resist the temptation to accede to another's desire out of fear of losing her. If you lose someone because you wouldn't be intimate early in the relationship, good riddance. All she wanted was the high of intimacy (sexual or otherwise), not *you*. Be willing to say, in response to a physical gesture of intimacy (sexual or romantic): "That felt really nice, but it's too early on for me to be comfortable with that kind of thing. Let's take it more slowly." Be willing to say, in response to a verbal expression of intimacy such as "I love you," "I want to be with you always," or "This was meant to be": "I appreciate that that's how you feel, but it's too early on for me to be comfortable with that kind of thing. Let's take it more slowly." Then, observe.

The Response

Watch what happens. If your lover or friend backs off and respects your discomfort by slowing down, terrific! He or she is letting you know he is attuned to and respects your needs. You have the opportunity to develop a mutually respecting and therefore trusting relationship. If he or she continues to pressure you, watch out! This individual is unresponsive to your stated needs, and may very well fail to respond to your other needs including the need for personal safety.

HIGH UP ON A PEDESTAL

Being put on a pedestal may feel great at the time, but all idols are bound to fall. And the higher the pedestal, the harder you will fall.

The Light of My Life

Take notice if the person has assigned you a position or qualities that are completely unrealistic given where you are in the relationship. For your new lover to say "You are the light of my life" or "You are everything to me" after two weeks of dating is scary. As flattering as such statements may be, they are impossible to live up to. Your lover knows too little about you at this point. Inevitably, he is projecting onto you all sorts of wonderful qualities you may or may not have.

Get off the Pedestal

Don't buy into the flattery. Enjoy the compliment, but respond to it in a way that lets the person clearly know you're not interested in climbing up onto that pedestal. Say, for example, nicely: "That's a really beautiful thing to say, but you know, I'm not comfortable with being the light of your life yet. We haven't had the opportunity to really get to know each other. For now, I'd rather just be 'a' light in your life, not the whole thing."

"Terrific," you say, "what a romance killer. Might as well just give him a list of all my faults and flaws and watch my new lover walk out the door." That's not what this is about. Trust your own worth. Know that being gently truthful with your lover from the beginning will enhance the development of the relationship, not destroy it. Allow your new lover to discover you over time, as you discover him. If that discovery is to be genuine, you need to be truthful about what unfolds. Love, romantic or platonic, is best built on genuine knowledge of each other. Love built on false hopes and dreams doesn't last. If correcting the person's statement so it is more in line with current reality as you experience it "kills the romance," then there wasn't a true romance there at all. There was just manipulation, a shallow replacement at best.

A Pedestal by Implication

Sometimes the pedestal is implied, not verbally acknowledged as stated earlier. This happens most frequently when a person behaves toward you as if you are all things to him: lover, best friend, constant companion. It's as if he has no life other than the one spent with you. Unfortunately, this degree of closeness is usually unhealthy at the beginning of a relationship. You just don't know each other well enough to be able to realistically fulfill all those needs. Abusive individuals don't care that you can't realistically fulfill all these needs; they will hold your failure to do so against you. After all, you did allow them to put you on that pedestal, and abusive individuals will hold you to that pedestal.

In the first few months of the relationship, do not allow yourself to be "everything" to your new lover. Don't give up your friends, hobbies, and private time, and don't encourage your new lover to give up his. Allow the closeness to grow with time, so it is grounded in genuine knowledge of the other and based on realistic expectations. That's great—and something to look forward to.

The Abuser's Need to Bond

Being "everything" to abusers often includes their need to have you "signed, sealed, and delivered" as early as possible. Their insecurity and pressing need to bond demands that you be "theirs" quickly. Faced with all that intensity, passive partners often say yes to commitments they are really not comfortable with rather than risk the loss of their new love.

Commitment comes in many shapes and sizes. Commitment in the beginning of a violent domestic relationship could be thought of as anything that implies permanence or exclusivity. Abusive individuals frequently press for sexual relations early in a relationship to cement the bond between you, implying exclusivity and hoping for permanence. Anne's orchestrating things so that she and Teri could be roommates quickly is another example of how an abusive individual might seek exclusivity and permanence.

Take Your Time

Don't let yourself be pressured by another's needs and demands. Take your time. If this is true love, it will be there tomorrow. Know yourself. An unwillingness to commit to a partner, sexually or otherwise, when you've been in the relationship six months is very different than an unwillingness to commit to a person you've only known two weeks. "Take your time" doesn't mean "Don't commit." It means "Don't go unthinkingly into an early commitment that you may later regret."

Assuming Commitment

Abusive individuals often assume commitment, meaning they behave as if you have a commitment, when in fact nothing has been discussed or agreed upon between you. A person who just starts leaving clothes at your place and staying there all the time, for example, is assuming a commitment. Passive partners are often reluctant to confront a lover with this kind of behavior, not wanting to scare the partner away. Allowing the assumed commitment to exist, however, signals to abusive individuals that you are willing to submit to their power and control and opens the way for other types of controlling behavior.

Be willing to talk about it. If your new friend, for example, is leaving clothes at your place and showing up all the time, talk about the commitment this kind of behavior assumes. Bring the assumption out into the open, so that it can cease to be an assumption, something that tends to get all of us in trouble. Talk openly about your desires, preferences, hopes, and fears about commitment at this stage of the relationship. Encourage your friend to speak openly as well. Any commitment the discussions lead to will be a mutually agreed-upon choice, with neither partner seeking to control the other.

It's OK to Say No

Don't be afraid to say no, fearing that if you don't give in to whatever the person wants you to commit to you'll lose them. If this is true love, both partners' readiness to commit must be taken into account. If your new lover is so desperate, so needy for commitment that the choice being offered within the first few months of a relationship is "Commit to me now or I walk," have the self-respect and courage to let him walk. Such a demand lets you know it wasn't you he wanted in the first place; all he wanted was a body to meet his needs, someone to do what he wanted when he wanted. That's not love—that's abuse.

THREE

The Hot Pursuit

ARE YOUR RIGHTS AND FEELINGS REALLY BEING RESPECTED?

In the midst of the intense good feelings that often mark the relationship's beginning, it's easy to overlook how an abuser in fact fails to respect your rights and feelings.

A Disrespectful Kiss

"How could John possibly have been not respecting my feelings?" Mary asked, astounded at my suggestion "I mean, in the beginning, all he wanted was to make me feel good! And I felt great!" "Yes," I said, "I know you did, and that's just the problem. Because you felt so terrific, you didn't see how inappropriate and disrespectful many of John's actions were." "For example?" Mary asked. "For example," I answered, "His taking your hand and kissing it when he picked up your envelope—he didn't check to see if you were married, or gay, or just plain not interested before doing that. This isn't Europe. Hand-kissing in building corridors isn't common here." "Oh," said Mary, "well, that's no big deal—I mean it was terribly romantic and he did apologize for doing it." "Yes, he apologized," I said, "and he got away with it—because it was so romantic. But how about later, when John pressured you to go to bed with him, was he respecting your feelings then?" I asked. Mary sighed, "No. No, he wasn't." "Do you feel you were clear with him about how you felt?" Mary thought for a moment, then in a tired voice said, "Yeah. I was clear about it. I was very clear about it. It just didn't seem to matter. I don't know, it . . . He just was so passionate!" "It's OK, Mary," I said gently, "don't blame yourself for giving in to him. No doubt he was wonderfully passionate. The important thing to see is that, passion or no passion, he was overriding your stated feelings. Just as in kissing your hand, he was ignoring how you might feel about it."

Lack of respect for the feelings and rights of others is a behavioral pattern common to abusers. Abusers typically have little or no regard for the feelings of others when they are under the influence of an internal push to get one of their needs met. People are usually so taken with all the affection and attention the abuser is giving them, however, that they fail to notice, as Mary did, just what's going on. When an abuser fails to respect your feelings about something small, like John's kissing Mary's hand, you assume it is because the matter is a small one. Not so. Failure to take the rights and feelings of others into account is a pattern. It's related to how abusers behave in the face of their own need, not to the size or importance of the situation.

Your Discomfort Is Ignored

Bob, given his previously limited sexual encounters, found Karen's sexual advances so appealing that he gave little attention to his discomfort with how she disregarded his feelings. His feelings of discomfort felt secondary to the passion Karen generated. "Sort of a fair trade-off," Bob told me. When Bob said the first thing Karen would say when she called was "I can feel your hands all over me, making me wet . . .," I asked him if that literally was what she said first. In other words, did she ever first check to see if it was a good time to talk, or if he was busy, or anything of the sort?

"No," Bob replied, looking at me incredulously, "Karen never even said 'Hello, how are you?'" "Did Karen ever call you at work?" I asked. "All the time," Bob said. "Did she ever ask you if that was comfortable or uncomfortable for you?" I asked. "Are you kidding?" said Bob. "Karen never asked me how I felt about things." "Did you ever tell her it made you uncomfortable?" I asked. "Well, I tried to at first," Bob said, "but she'd interrupt, she'd say something even more outrageous, and I'd get so stimulated I'd forget all about being uncomfortable with her calling like that." "Did you ever drop something you were doing to go over and see her?" I continued. "All the time," Bob said. "Was it ever inconvenient for you to drop everything and go over there?" I asked. "Sure," Bob said. "Did you tell her that?" "Sure, lots of times," Bob replied, "but Karen didn't care, she just wanted me there." I looked at Bob, saying nothing. A moment passed.

"It's funny," Bob said ruefully, "I thought it was really great Karen never talked about feelings. I mean, I wasn't getting all that pressure women usually give you about wanting to know your feelings and stuff like that. I never thought before right now how little she cared about how I felt. But you're right, if I said something about how difficult it was to just drop everything and come over, she'd laugh and do something wildly sexy and I'd forget all about it." Feelings are important. Certainly in a relationship, both partners' feelings are important.

Another way Karen systematically ignored Bob's feelings was in the sexual arena itself. The refrain Karen repeated endlessly was "I want you, you're the greatest." This sexual flattery deafened Bob's ears to the fact that Karen's romancing of him was all based on what he did for her, how satisfied he made *her* feel. She expressed no concern for his wishes, desires, or satisfactions, but simply behaved as if whatever she was doing to and for him was fine by him. The fact that Bob was indeed very satisfied and very much enjoying Karen's sexual prowess should in no way diminish the fact that Karen failed to demonstrate either interest in or caring for Bob's feelings. Her blatant disregard for Bob's feelings in this area is part of a larger pattern of general disregard for Bob's feelings.

Your Time Is Their Time

Because abusers are so charming in the beginning phases, most of us don't see the lack of respect. Certainly Peter didn't. Peter was much too impressed by Tony when he turned up at his door with a picnic basket to point out to Tony that it would have been more appropriate to find out ahead of time if Peter was available that evening. It wasn't until much later in the relationship that Peter realized Tony's complete lack of regard for his feelings.

Your Rights Are Ignored

Teri was so captivated by Anne's amazing abilities that she didn't see Anne's flagrant lack of respect for her rights and feelings until much later in the friendship, yet the pattern was obvious early on. To break Teri's lease without discussing it with her first is a rampant disregard of Teri's rights to conduct her life as she sees fit. It is truly a violation, an act that shows complete lack of consideration for Teri's feelings. What if Teri wanted to stay in her present apartment until her lease was up? What if she wanted some time to think it over? What if Teri couldn't afford a different living arrangement? Anne took none of these possibilities into consideration. Driven by her internal push to have her needs met, Anne overlooked how Teri might feel about the situation. It's only much later that Teri would realize that the pattern of disrespect had actually started in those first few weeks.

"I WANT WHAT I WANT WHEN I WANT IT": ABUSERS HAVE TROUBLE WITH IMPULSE CONTROL

In the beginning of the relationship, everything feels wonderfully spontaneous. He calls at odd hours, she drops by with a present or just to say hi. There is in this a marvelous breaking of the rules, a certain delicious sense of freedom. You never know quite what to expect, but at this stage of the relationship, the unexpected is always something delightful and people don't consider the implications. People do not see how the lover's or friend's dropping by unannounced at this early stage presumes a depth of relationship that does not yet exist. Nor do they see that the lover's or friend's spontaneity reflects a lack of impulse control that will later become one of the abuser's forms of control.

The Abuser's Emotions and Needs

Abusers are generally unaware of their own emotions and needs until those emotions and needs are intense. The pressure of their emotions is so great that by the time abusers do become aware, they tend to respond in extreme fashion. Physical violence is frequently an abuser's extreme response, however inappropriate, to extreme internal pressures. For abusers one of the most important elements of successfully overcoming their violence is getting in touch with their emotions and needs early enough to channel those emotions and needs constructively. For example, in therapy, abusers learn to feel the onset of their anger when it is at a very mild stage, enabling them to express their anger verbally rather than through violent action.

The needs of abusers at the beginning of a relationship are to connect, to be close, to bond with the chosen other. These needs are every bit as intense as the need to release anger, which will come later in the relationship. Abusers tend to act upon their needs immediately. In the beginning, that impulsivity usually takes on some pleasant form, such as telephone calls or, as with Mary, a kiss on the hand.

The Kiss on Mary's Hand

Because the kiss on her hand was, for her, charming and romantic, Mary didn't think about what that behavior might mean in the larger scheme of things. And certainly, by itself, a kiss on the hand is just that—a kiss! But the way in which that kiss was delivered should raise a warning flag— albeit a small one. It is a warning to pay attention to other examples of poor impulse control that John might exhibit. After all, Mary did not offer her hand to be kissed, nor was she in a situation where that might be expected behavior, such as at a party or other social situation. John simply took Mary's hand, which was reaching to take back her envelope (not reaching out for him), and kissed it.

As small as this incident may seem, it is an example of poor impulse control. John acted on his need of the moment, without considering the consequences or appropriateness of his actions. John's poor impulse control was also evident in his need to have sex with Mary despite her clear statements to him that she was not ready for such intimacy. The pressure of his need overrode his ability to think through the consequences of his behavior.

Poor impulse control is frightening. Individuals who can't, for example, prevent themselves from touching a stranger in an inappropriate manner or stop themselves from behaving in a way that is very uncomfortable for their partner, may very well have trouble preventing themselves from hitting a loved one.

Sexual Impulsiveness

Karen's lack of impulse control showed in a very different area. It may seem every man's dream to have a woman call and start the conversation with explicit sexual conversation, but the fact is, there was no conversation. Karen wasn't calling in order to talk *with* Bob. Karen was acting impulsively, responding to her pressing internal need regardless of how her actions might affect Bob. Karen didn't give Bob the room to reply. As soon as she had made her urgent need known, she hung up.

Such spontaneous sexual openness can be thrilling, if within the boundaries of what is comfortable for both parties. Despite Bob's letting her know how inconvenient such calls were for him, Karen's lack of impulse control was demonstrated when she continued to make the calls nonetheless, unable or unwilling to channel her sexual impulses in a way that could still be thrilling, but also acceptable to both parties.

Surprise Visits

When I asked Peter how he felt about Tony's unannounced arrival on his doorstep with the picnic basket, he said, "It's funny, I felt two things at the same time, incredibly pleased and excited on the one hand, and kind of intruded upon on the other." "You look puzzled," I commented. "Well, yes," Peter said, "I mean it's such a nice thing to do—surprise me with something I really like. I don't know why it made me kind of uncomfortable." "What did you do with that feeling?" I asked. "Forgot it, pushed it aside," Peter answered. "Didn't talk to Tony about it?" I asked. "No," Peter said, "I just thought it was me being weird."

Peter's reaction is a common one. Passive partners in a violent domestic relationship often attribute their initial discomfort with the active partner's poor impulse control to their own "weirdness." After all, how can you be upset with someone for fulfilling a fantasy? It's all too easy under such delicious circumstances to push aside the uncomfortable feelings generated by the abuser's intrusiveness. During the early stage of a relationship, respect for the other's privacy is important. At the very least the person dropping by should say something along the lines of: "I thought I'd surprise you with a picnic. Are you busy? Is this a good time? Is this something you would like to do?"

When I asked Peter if Tony had asked any of those questions, Peter laughed, "Tony never asked if I wanted to do something he wanted to do. He either grabbed me and off we went, or got pissed if I wouldn't go along. Ask me? Oh, please."

The Damage of Impulsiveness

Anne not only failed to ask Teri if it was all right for Anne to break Teri's lease, Anne did not rein in her impulses long enough to consider the potentially damaging consequences of her action on Teri's life. What if Teri could not afford the new apartment, had lost her first-and-last month's rent, or had been unable to afford all the charges of turning on new utilities, telephone lines, and other such services? Teri would have been at very real financial risk. The extent to which Anne acted on her impulse in this situation should have given Teri pause. People tend to act in ways consistent with themselves. If Anne acted this strongly on one impulse, the likelihood was she would act just as strongly on another, with the same disregard for consequences, however damaging. The fact that Anne's behavior did not strike Teri as inappropriate attests to the frightening drug-like quality of the initial attention and affection of an abuser.

"NOW YOU SEE IT, NOW YOU DON'T": THE DISTRACTING MANEUVER

Charm

"He was so charming," Mary said of John. "Half the time I wasn't paying attention to what he was doing because the way he was doing it was so charming!" "What do you mean?" I asked. "Well, like when he kissed my hand, that first day. When I think about it now, I remember feeling startled, and like he'd conned me into it. I mean, I was reaching out for my envelope, and it was like what magicians do—you know—you're looking at one thing and 'presto!' something else happens. Suddenly my hand was being kissed. I remember pulling back, but then he blushed and stammered and dropped my hand real quick and said, 'I shouldn't have done that, I shouldn't have said that, I'm sorry, I'm sorry.' He was so adorable, I forgave him on the spot. I forgot all about how startled I had been and that feeling of being somehow conned, it just left. Now I wish it hadn't."

That's what charm does. It makes you forget, distracts you from what is really going on. This is not to say that charm isn't delicious, delightful, pleasing, and wonderful, and is to be enjoyed. But be on the alert; abusers tend to use charm as a distraction from otherwise intrusive or inappropriate behavior.

"He did the same thing the first time we made love," Mary said. "I was uncomfortable, I kept telling John I wasn't ready, but he just kept kissing me so nicely, and saying sweet things in my ear, he was so utterly romantic, I got all caught up in the romance of it. I felt like I was in a dream, it wasn't real and somehow that made it OK." John was very effective in distracting Mary from her own discomfort and from the pushiness of his behavior that would later become violence.

Outrageous Sexuality

Karen was masterful at distracting Bob from the inappropriateness of her behavior. "When Karen walked into my office the day I got transferred," Bob said, "my first thought was wow, what a beautiful woman! But when she hopped up and sat on the side of my desk, I thought, What are you doing? My office is glass-walled on the front, right in the middle of a busy area, and this was in the middle of a work day. Plus I was surprised and put off—it was too close, too invasive, but then she smiled and started talking real seductively and suddenly she was off my desk again. It all happened so fast, I hardly knew what hit me. I remember just sitting there, stunned.

The fact that she had made real overt sexual insinuations when she had no idea if I was married, single, spoken for, or what, sat on the papers on my desk and all that, just vanished. I was completely taken by her coming on to me. She could have walked away with 20 files, I probably wouldn't have noticed."

As outrageous as Karen's distracting sexuality is, it is not uncommon. Abusers are intense. The pressure of their internal need is such that abusers tend to be intense regardless of how that need gets expressed, as seductiveness or assault. The intensity of their distracting maneuvers is usually equal to the inappropriateness of their behavior. The bigger the inappropriateness, the bigger the distraction.

Head in the Clouds

"When Tony said I was the best thing that ever happened to him I was blown away by how special and wanted that made me feel. I didn't even consider what he was up to," Peter said. "What was Tony up to?" I asked. "Moving into my life," Peter replied. "Becoming my one and only. We never talked about it; Tony just assumed that if he wanted to be with me forever, I'd want it too. Anytime I'd bring up that maybe we were going a little too fast here, and we really didn't know that much about each other, and like that, he would be so darned seductive. Not sexually as much as with words and gestures that made me feel special, cherished, treasured. I'd forget all about my concerns. How could any of that matter when someone was making me feel so special?"

How, indeed? It's hard to keep your feet on the ground when your head is in the clouds. Yet it does matter. Peter's concerns were legitimate and needed to be addressed, not pushed aside with Tony's distracting maneuvers.

Doing the Impossible

Anne's distraction of Teri took a very similar form to Tony's: Anne's "bedazzling" Teri with her impossible feat of breaking the lease and finding a new apartment quickly was just as effective as Tony's "bedazzling" Peter with tender words.

YOU SIGNAL THAT YOU ARE RECEPTIVE

Distracting maneuvers serve two purposes for abusers: to distract from inappropriate behavior and to check the passive partner's receptivity to, or allowance of, inappropriate behavior. As I said in the preface, it takes two people to create a violent domestic relationship—an active and a passive partner. In the beginning of a relationship, abusers "test" the willingness of an individual to be a passive partner by engaging in mildly inappropriate behavior and seeing how the person reacts. If the person becomes distracted by choice, and thus tacitly accepts the inappropriate behavior, abusers will take this response as "permission" to do more of the same.

Too Quick to Forgive

John's quick apology, upon letting go of Mary's hand, was a way for him to find out how receptive Mary would be to his level of intensity. He could also judge how easily she could be won over by such romantic behavior and how easily she would forgive or be distracted from inappropriate or invasive behavior. Her willingness to easily and quickly forgive him told John that Mary was susceptible to intense romantic gestures, would probably overlook inappropriate behavior, and would probably allow him to develop the relationship his way.

His subsequent "testing," certainly the most critical up until that point, was to see if he could get Mary to have sex with him even though she was uncomfortable and felt unready. "So by giving in to his romancing me, and sleeping with him, I let John know I would give in on other things," said Mary. "Yes," I replied, "unfortunately so."

Failing to Set Boundaries

Similarly, Karen's seductive behavior served both to distract Bob from how inconsiderate she was of his time and work obligations and to see how willing he was to be so distracted. When you let a person override your boundaries, you let her know that you're willing to let her be in charge of setting your boundaries for you—a dangerous allowance to give to anyone.

Not Standing Up for Oneself

Tony tested Peter's receptivity by dropping in without announcing his visit or prefacing it with a request for time together. Tony continued to test by moving into Peter's life and distracting Peter from bringing up concerns about how the relationship was developing. In both cases, Peter's inability or unwillingness to stand up for his feelings of discomfort gave Tony tacit permission to keep on ignoring those feelings. After all, if Peter wasn't willing to stand up for himself, why should Tony?

Giving Free Rein

Anne had been checking Teri's receptivity all along, with her invitations to do things together, talk on the phone long hours, and so forth. Teri's willingness to go out with her and spend time together certainly signaled Teri's general availability. What really told Anne that Teri would allow Anne to indulge in inappropriate behavior was Teri's complete and unqualified acceptance of Anne's breaking of Teri's lease. In a sense, Teri was communicating to Anne that Anne could do whatever she liked with Teri's life. Anne proceeded to do exactly that.

A ONE-SIZE-FITS-ALL SEDUCTIVE APPROACH

Cookie-Cutter Romance

"Sometimes I got the feeling, with John, that he'd done this a lot before," Mary said. "Done what before?" I asked. "Well, I got this funny feeling that he'd said the same romantic words before—a lot," Mary explained, "that he'd brought a single red rose on every date before, like his gestures were cookie-cutter." "Like he had one approach to romancing someone and you were getting the standard treatment?" I asked. "Yes," Mary replied, "as if it almost didn't matter who I was, what mattered was his romancing." "What gave you that feeling, Mary?" I asked, wanting to know more. Mary thought for a moment. "I don't really like red roses," Mary laughed. "I know that sounds funny, but I don't. I like pink roses, but really I prefer other flowers. I told John that, in as nice a way as I could, but it was like that didn't matter. He said something like 'yes, but red roses are the heart of romance, you'll see' and just kept on giving me red roses. I felt it would be real ungrateful to say anything again, but it did bother me." She paused a moment, remembering. "And you know," Mary continued, "John was like that about a lot of things. I'd tell him I preferred to be caressed a certain way, and he'd do it that way one time, then he'd go back to how he liked to caress me and try to convince me I'd like it better too eventually. Or he'd call me sweetie, which I hate, and it didn't seem to matter how many times I told him that word had very unpleasant memories for me. He'd keep right on using it until I gave up and didn't mention it any more. It's like he had one way of doing things and I had to either like it or lump it."

Abusers are bound in the intensity of their own needs and emotions. It is very difficult for them to empathize with another. Abusers are generally so driven to take care of themselves that to shift course and somehow take care of themselves while considering the needs of others is almost impossible. They tend to develop standard well-rehearsed ways of dealing with people in a variety of situations and stick to those ways regardless of the other's input.

Generic Sexuality

Bob experienced Karen's sexuality as following the same one-size-fits-all approach. "It was like Karen had decided what turned guys on, and that's what she did," Bob said. "And she was right, what she did was a huge turn-on, but people are different, you know? Some of the things I like sexually are different from what Karen would do naturally. But whenever I would suggest something— and I'm not talking about S&M or anything like that—I mean just changing to a different position or maybe doing more of one activity and less of another, Karen wouldn't pay any attention at all. She'd just laugh and keep right on doing what she was doing. Sure, she was the greatest in bed, but sometimes I got this eerie feeling like it wouldn't matter who was in bed with her. I used to have fantasies about it, that I'd get my buddy to change places with me in the middle of things and Karen would keep right on going. But it wasn't a nice fantasy. It made me feel empty, like I was just another guy to her, nobody special, that she'd be the same with everybody."

The Apparently Personalized Approach

Although the one-size-fits-all approach is by far the most common, there are variations on the theme. Peter experienced a very different approach in the beginning of his relationship with Tony. The picnic basket experience exemplifies the apparently personalized approach. Tony paid very close attention to Peter's need to be special and presented him with experiences that answered that need. However, Tony did not ask Peter what he would most enjoy in terms of such experiences. "It's like Tony had a set repertoire," Peter said. "It was either the surprise gift, or the surprise dinner, or the surprise event. So even though it seemed personal, like he was really thinking of me and what would make me feel good, I always had this odd feeling that it really wasn't. It was strange."

Anne also used an apparently more personalized approach, offering Teri invitations to concerts and movies she knew Teri was interested in. However, Anne did not deviate from an approach of such invitations, nor did she look to Teri for suggestions on what else might please her. "I sometimes thought that Anne was buying my company with her invitations. I didn't care, really—she earned more than I did and I couldn't have gone with her as much if I had been paying my share. But what was funny is she didn't seem to realize that at the time, I would have hung out with her anyway, even if we just sat at home watching a video. That would have been just as much fun for me. She just had this one way she liked to do things together, you know, go out—so OK! What the heck. I had a good time."

FOUR

How to Get the Respect You Deserve

RESPECTING YOUR RIGHTS AND FEELINGS

An abusive individual in the beginning of a relationship is an intensely focused individual. Such intense focus actually constitutes much of the abusive individual's initial charm. Intensity is, for many people, very attractive, as evidenced by the many hit movies and other media that capitalize on the immense drawing power of intensity. The focal point of abusers' intensity is satisfaction of their need to merge as completely as possible with another. In the service of this need, abusive individuals will do whatever it takes. Abusers are often so charming or so seductive in how they go about getting what they want that you either don't notice or are too enchanted to care about the fact that they are not taking your feelings into account. It may *seem* like it because all that charm and seduction makes you feel so good, but actually, one has nothing to do with the other.

The Pull of Intensity

For example, your new love says, "I love you, you're the most wonderful woman in the world. I can't believe how lucky I am to have found you" and your heart sings. You say, "Oh, me too, but you can't keep calling me at work, I'll get in trouble." Your love says, "Oh, I know, I'm sorry, I just can't help myself, I just had to hear your voice. I couldn't wait until tonight." "Tonight?" you ask, surprised. You'd planned on doing the laundry and kicking back, watching TV tonight. "Yes, tonight, I miss you so much already," your love says, then hesitates and in an injured tone asks, "Don't you want to see me tonight?" "Oh, of course," you say, suddenly alert and afraid to lose this wonderful person who apparently adores you. How can you refuse so much love? The laundry can wait, and you can watch TV some other night. "See, Dr. Noelle," you tell me, "see how much he loves me?"

"No," I say reluctantly, not wanting to burst your balloon but having to. "No, what I see is you're caught in the feelings being generated by the budding relationship, but your new love is not respecting any of your feelings." "Explain!" you demand, annoyed."You asked him not to call you at work, correct?" I ask. "Correct," you say, still annoyed. "He did anyway, correct?" I ask. "Yes," you say. "You had no plans to see each other that night, did you?" "No, we didn't," you respond. "But he expected you to spend the evening together, right? And when you seemed surprised, he manipulates you with an injured tone into saying yes. He didn't ask you if you had other plans, or were tired, or anything else, right?" Silence. You sigh.

Your Feelings Ignored

Abusive individuals may make you feel good, but they don't take your feelings into account at all. They either bulldoze through your feelings with their need or ignore your feelings completely, whichever tactic is most likely to work. John bulldozed past Mary's reluctance to sleep with him early on. Tony ignored how Peter might feel about his quasi move-in. Anne ignored how Teri might feel about breaking Teri's lease. And as long as you're feeling "high" on the relationship, you are all too likely to allow your feelings to go by the wayside.

People are often afraid to express their true feelings in the beginning of a relationship lest they risk losing their new lover or friend. Unfortunately, if you are afraid of losing someone early in the relationship, you are far too likely to sacrifice your feelings, your wants, needs, and preferences to theirs, which in the end means you will not have a mutually satisfying relationship. A dear friend of mine often says,"It is better to fight a lot in the beginning of a relationship than assume all is bliss and be devastated in the end." This is not to suggest that fighting for the sake of fighting is good, but it implies that it is better to fight for the expression of your feelings than to consistently allow your feelings to be run over or ignored.

Manipulating Your Emotions

In addition to ignoring or bulldozing past your feelings in the service of their needs, abusive individuals also deliberately manipulate you into a certain emotional state for their own ends. For example, Karen would talk sexily over the phone to Bob because she wanted sex right then. If the way you feel about certain things and your preferences happen to coincide with what the abuser wants, all is well. For example, as long as Bob was willing to drop everything and run to fulfill her, everything went fine; their feelings coincided. Otherwise, too bad, your feelings don't count. When Bob didn't run right over, Karen would explode.

Acknowledge Your Feelings

Acknowledge *all* of your feelings. Many of us, caught in the throes of passion, put our other feelings on the back burner. It is important to stay in touch with yourself, to ask yourself from time to time, "How do I feel about this? Am I comfortable about that?" and not dismiss your feelings. If you do not respect your feelings, how can you expect someone else to respect your feelings? It is vital to the successful development of a healthy relationship to be aware of and respect your feelings regarding the various events and issues that come up in the relationship.

Your feelings are important and should matter to the people who are closest to you. Don't let someone's charm, intensity, or passion overwhelm your feelings.

Express Your Feelings

A person cannot respect your feelings if you do not express them. Don't expect the other person will just know what to do or understand how you'll feel. Wearing rose-colored glasses in the beginning of a relationship could be lethal. Often, as a passive partner you are afraid of expressing your feelings because you don't want to rock the "happiness" boat. "Gosh," you say to yourself, "if I tell her again I don't like it when she calls at work, I'll probably hurt her feelings, or she might not call at all anymore. That would be awful." So you don't say anything. Now, not only have you made it impossible for the other person to respect your feelings (because she doesn't know what they are), you've also deprived yourself of the opportunity to see if this individual would respect your feelings if she *did* know what they were. Don't assume that because someone is paying you compliments and giving you attention or being romantic that she is full of good intentions. You have no idea what her true intentions are at this point.

Be willing to express your feelings. If your lover or friend genuinely cares about you, she will be willing to listen to how you feel and to work with you on an issue. Stand up for yourself when your feelings are not taken into consideration. Be willing to say, for example, "I don't like it when people come unannounced to my home. Please call first to see if it's a good time for you to come over," or "It's not convenient for me for you to come over tonight, let's plan a different time together," or "As much as I like to talk to you, please don't call me at work unless it's an emergency." "Oh my gosh," you say, "I could never say that, that's so cold." Fine. Then develop a warmer way of saying it, but say it! Cold is a lot better than dead.

The Spontaneity Objection

Don't give in to protestations of spontaneity. If your lover or friend says, "I like to be spontaneous, I like to just do things unplanned," then respond with "That's great— then just spontaneously call me from the corner pay phone, but please call me first," or "Spontaneous is great, when we're out together and we just do whatever we feel like, but spontaneously turning up at my workplace doesn't support me at my job, so please don't do it."

What's the Response?

Once you've been clear about expressing your feelings, observe how the person responds. If you say, for example, "I'm uncomfortable having sex with you this early in the relationship," notice how your partner deals with that information. If he keeps trying to persuade you to have sex, despite your clear statement of how you feel about it, that's a danger signal. If you tell your lover or friend, as in the earlier examples, that you don't want him to call at work, or drop by, or whatever it is that feels inappropriate or uncomfortable to you, observe how he deals with your feelings. Abusive individuals may pay lip-service to your feelings but will not alter their behavior to take your feelings into account.

Don't excuse the person on the grounds that you liked what he or she did anyhow. Maybe you did, and that's fine. For example, you may discover you like spontaneous visits at work or that you are glad your lover or friend was persistent about moving in, despite your reluctance. What is important here is not whether you end up doing what the other prefers, but to observe whether the person respects and honors how you feel about things in your life. That's what tells you if you're dealing with an abusive individual.

POOR IMPULSE CONTROL

Abusive individuals do what they want to do when they want to do it without stopping to consider the consequences of their actions. Their internal push is so strong, they want what they want *now*, and have very little ability to delay satisfaction. Such lack of impulse control contributes to the passionate intensity of their pursuit of you, but it also contributes to the passionate intensity of their violence when it erupts. It is important for you to be able to evaluate your lover or friend's ability to handle these impulses early on in the relationship.

Life without Passion?

"Oh, great," you say to yourself, "I have to accept a boring life without passion, so as not to risk domestic violence." Fortunately, you don't have to go about it that way, since (thankfully!) not all individuals who are passionate are also critically lacking in impulse control. Once you know how to assess lack of impulse control, you can find a passionate individual who can temper impulses as is appropriate.

"I Want" versus "I Need"

An impulse can be thought of as an instinctive "I want." "I want" is a preferential response to the more basic "I need." For example, "I want a soda" is a preferential response to "I'm thirsty, I *need* liquid," since clearly many other substances besides a soda would quench your thirst. "I want to marry a rich person" is a preferential response to "I *need* security" for some people. For others, the preferential response to "I need security" might be "I want to find a stable job." We start off in life with "I want" as the motivating force behind everything. Babies, for example, have great purity of "I want." Nothing but that "I want" matters, as any parent of a 2-year-old knows. However, through the years, we learn to temper "I want" with an appreciation for the consequences of "I want." For example, the early "I want to pull the cat's tail" gets tempered with "I want to pull the cat's tail, but if I do, Mother and Father will scold me." Later, we say, "I want a lot of money, so I think I'll rob a bank." This gets tempered (for most of us) with, "Yeah, I'd love the money, but I'm not a robber, I'd probably get caught, and besides, I'd feel bad about doing that kind of thing." So, you don't. You've learned to control your impulses.

Thinking about Consequences

It should be obvious from these examples that controlling your impulses has a great deal to do with your ability and willingness to think through the negative consequences of your actions. Abusive individuals are often severely inhibited in their ability to appropriately weigh negative consequences. This is a pattern of behavior that shows up whenever such an individual is faced with "I want." You can tell a great deal about how a person will deal with violent impulses such as a desire to lash out from how that individual deals with more pleasant impulses, such as impulsively wanting to buy things or go places.

Dealing with Impulses

Observe how your lover or friend deals with her impulses, generally speaking. For example, when she wants to buy something costly, does she think about how that purchase will affect her finances? Does she think about the item for a day or two, or longer, or does she buy it on the spur of the moment? Does she think about how the item fits with the rest of her lifestyle? Or does she buy whatever she wants, without regard to the consequences, and then have to scramble to deal with the cost of the purchase? "Does this mean," you ask, worried, "that if I buy something on impulse I'm a potentially abusive individual?" No, of course not. Many people who buy impulsively are not abusive. However, buying things impulsively can be a warning sign of abusive behavior when it is found in the context of a larger pattern of behaviors such as blaming or disrespect of feelings.

Handling Frustration

Persons who have poor impulse control also have difficulty dealing with the frustration of their impulses.

Let's say your friend wants to go to a certain movie. That movie is sold out. Observe how your friend deals with the frustration of this impulse. Does she figure out an enjoyable alternative, such as going to a later show or seeing a different movie down the block? Or does she allow her frustration full expression and either pout or get angry? The way your friend deals with the ordinary frustrations of life will tell you a great deal about how she is likely to deal with you when something you do or say frustrates her. Don't excuse her pout or anger as "Oh, she really wanted to see that movie, hey, I'd get pissed too." Instead, note it as something to pay attention to. Be willing to observe more closely, perhaps, how your friend deals with other frustrations.

Spontaneity Objection

Don't get duped into the idea that being impulsive is somehow spontaneous or creative and that you're an old stick in the mud if being impulsive doesn't seem very acceptable to you. Not thinking ahead to the consequences of our actions is what too often leads to bankruptcy, unwanted pregnancies, and failed marriages. Spontaneity is great as long as there is at least some thought given to the consequences. For example, knowing you have budgeted $50 (and therefore thought through the consequences) to spend on something fun for yourself, you can now spontaneously spend it on whatever strikes your fancy. Creativity has nothing whatsoever to do with impulsiveness. You may begin a creative act with the impulse "I want to paint" or "I want to design something" or "I want to invent something" but much of creativity is the often lengthy and complex imaginative process that then ensues.

Trust Your Comfort Zone

Stand your ground. If your lover wants you to do something impulsive or does something impulsive and you don't feel comfortable with the impulsive quality, even if the action in and of itself isn't objectionable to you, let your lover know. State clearly, "I love to play hooky from work occasionally, but I'm not comfortable doing it on the spur of the moment without at least thinking if it's an OK day to play hooky. If it's not, I'd rather play hooky another day." Notice how the person responds. If he is disappointed but says "Well, OK, I understand" and then is amenable to figuring out when playing hooky would be acceptable to you, great! If, however, he pressures you to go along with his impulse, or gets extremely frustrated and angry, take it as a warning sign. Continue to stand your ground, but be aware that your lover has problems in the area of impulse control, and therefore may have problems keeping violent tendencies in check.

Don't let yourself be influenced by the person's disapproval. It's tempting to go along with a significant other's desires to win his or her approval. If your lover's approval hinges on your doing something that is uncomfortable or damaging to you, that approval is not being given to you for being who you are. The approval is being given to you for performing according to your lover's preferences. You are not a trained seal. Don't act like one! If the person qualifies you as "no fun" for wanting to give some thought about whether it's a good hooky day, watch out. He or she probably has poor impulse control.

DISTRACTING MANEUVERS

Abusers have a way of getting your attention off their inconsiderateness, poor impulse control, and other inappropriate behaviors by charming, seducing, or otherwise distracting you. The easiest way to identify such a distraction is to stay in touch with your sense of what feels right to you, and respect that.

State Your Feelings

If you feel even for a moment that your rights, your feelings, or your preferences are not being taken into account, let your lover know how you feel. Don't allow the distraction to take your attention off the inappropriate behavior. For example, your lover tells a friend of yours, without consulting you first, that you are unavailable for lunch. When you find out and confront him with it, he says, "Oh, you've spoiled my surprise, I was going to take you to lunch. That's why I told your friend you weren't available," and proceeds to charm you with where he is going to take you and how much fun it will be and wouldn't you rather spend the time with him anyway. Don't give in to the distraction. Be willing to address the behavior he is trying to cover up. Say, for example: "You're being so charming that I would just love to go along with you on this, but I'm not happy with how you didn't check out with me how I'd feel about this before doing it."

Responding to Your Objection

Notice how the person responds to your objection. Does he just intensify the distraction? Or does he back off and say, "I'm sorry, I didn't think to ask you that, that was inconsiderate of me" and then discuss how you felt about his behavior and how each of you would like to handle a similar situation in the future? If he intensifies the distraction, saying, for example, "Oh, you know I'm only think-ing of you. I wanted to surprise you and make you feel really special. Here you are spoiling the whole thing, making me feel bad," there's a problem. Your lover is getting even further away from what happened by dis-tracting you with guilt. Try to get back to the original hurt, his canceling of your plans, and deal with that. If you are again unsuccessful, realize that you are involved with some-one who is more interested in controlling your life than in creating a relationship *with* you. That's a warning sign.

Excusing the Distraction

If your lover intensifies his distraction, don't let him off the hook by saying to yourself, "Oh, it's not that important, I didn't care that much about that anyway." In so doing, you are contributing to his disrespect of your feelings. In the beginning of a relationship, you set the ground rules for how that relationship will function. If you start by saying your partner's inattention to your feelings and preferences doesn't matter, you may end up suffering his indifference to your pain as he batters you.

"But Dr. Noelle," you say, "everybody does some-thing wrong and tries to tap dance their way out of it once in a while— nobody's perfect!" It's not about perfect, it's about patterns of behavior. If your lover does something inappropriate once in a great while and tries to distract you out of objecting, it's not a big deal. It is preferable to talk about it at some point, yes, but more importantly, try to determine if there's a pattern. Put yourself in observa-tion mode. How often does your lover try to distract you? Is this something that happens every time your lover does something you find uncomfortable? Is your lover open to discussing this type of behavior? These are the sorts of questions to ask yourself.

CHECKING RECEPTIVITY

Abusers don't just walk up to someone and say, "Are you willing to be abused? Will you promise to stay with me even if I alternately adore and beat you?" It wouldn't work, most of us would run away as fast as our legs would carry us. Yet people do fall in love with and stay with abusive individuals, often long after the violence has begun. How do abusers find out who is open to such a relationship?

Minor Violations Matter

Abusive individuals check your receptivity, they "test" you on how willing you are to let your rights and feelings be violated by seeing how you respond to minor violations of your rights and feelings. This process is largely unconscious on the part of the abuser, but that doesn't make it any less real, nor any less dangerous for you.

Many of us are so hungry for love that we mistake the intensity and attention abusers lavish on us at the beginning of the relationship for love. Wanting to keep that feeling going, wanting to keep the love, passive partners allow abusers to get away with many small violations of the passive partner's rights and feelings. Each time you allow your lover to ignore, discount, or run over your rights and feelings, you are sending them an unmistakable message: "Hey, no problem, I can take it. Go ahead, ignore my feelings, violate my rights, I'm strong, I'll still love you." Each time you allow another such violation, you reinforce that message. Eventually, abusers, having repeatedly tested your willingness to have your rights and feelings walked on, feel safe in upping the ante. And so they do, until one day you are hit, kicked, shoved, or pushed and wonder what the heck just happened.

Speak Your Truth

Be proactive. Stand up for yourself. If you don't like something someone says or does, let them know *now*, early on, the first time it happens. You don't have to be angry, mean, or nasty about it, you can simply say, for example, "I'm uncomfortable breaking plans with a friend. My friends are important to me. Please don't ask that of me," or "Please don't tell my friends I'm not here when you pick up the phone and I am here. That's very uncomfortable for me," or "Please don't rearrange my things, I like them the way I have arranged them." Then, watch what happens. Is your friend willing to talk about it? Does she apologize and refrain from repeating that behavior? Or does she apologize for the behavior and do it again anyway? If the latter, the abuser is once again checking your receptivity. This is not a good sign, be aware of it and react accordingly.

Forgive Slowly

Don't be quick to forgive someone doing something that is uncomfortable for you because you're afraid of losing the relationship. If you're involved in the beginnings of a violent domestic relationship, it is best you *do* lose the relationship. Once you've pointed out what distressed you, if your friend apologizes, don't say "Oh, that's OK" and brush aside your own discomfort. Learn to say "I appreciate your apology. Thank you for not doing it again." This lets your partner know you're serious about having your rights and feelings respected.

Nonabusive individuals will try their best to respect your rights and feelings. You will not only keep the relationship, it will deepen as you give the other the opportunity to see more of the genuine you.

Remember you are in the beginning phases of this relationship. What you allow as acceptable behavior in the beginning is what will remain acceptable throughout. Don't let it be acceptable to ignore your feelings and rights. If you do, that's exactly what you're in for down the line.

ONE-SIZE-FITS-ALL SEDUCTIONS

Abusers don't respond to other people as separate entities, individuals with their own hopes, dreams, expectations, and desires. Abusers tend to respond to others as food, as something for them to consume according to their needs. That's why many people who have been in an abusive relationship feel drained, as if they've been sucked dry by an emotional vampire. The analogy is unfortunately a good one. Abusers suck the very heart and soul out of people, and in the most extreme cases, their very life.

The Hook

Because abusers don't see other people as people, but as objects for consumption, they don't seek relationships in the true sense of the word. They seek power and control. Abusive individuals rely on manipulation, a prime tool of power and control, to bring you into a relationship with them. Abusive individuals tend to assume that whatever manipulation worked to hook one person will work to hook another. Therefore they rely on one-size-fits-all romantic or seductive gestures to entice you into a relationship.

It is perfectly normal that at the *very* beginning of a relationship, before an individual knows your preferences, his romantic or seductive gestures are going to be stereotypical. As time goes on, however, observe. Does your new lover seek to explore and discover what your personal preferences are? Does he alter, tailor or adapt his beginning approaches with those preferences in mind?

Express Your Preferences

Passive partners have a tendency to accept whatever romantic or seductive gestures their lover is proffering, not wanting to hurt the other one's feelings, or fearful of putting a damper on the relationship. This is a dangerous tendency! Don't lie or otherwise pretend that a generic romantic or seductive gesture pleases you unless it really does. Express your appreciation of the gesture to the degree that you enjoy it, and let your lover know what you really like.

"Oh, great," you say, "how do you tell someone who just took you to a fancy restaurant that you hate fancy restaurants? All he was doing was trying to please me!" You say it nicely, for example: "I am so touched you took me to the Ritzy Restaurant. It was a terrific experience! But you know what I really like—going to double features. I know this sounds insane, but I find nothing more romantic than sitting through a double feature stuffing my face with popcorn. Does that seem totally strange to you?" Now you've opened the discussion to what you like, and the two of you can talk about each other's preferences.

As you let the person know your preferences, pay attention. Does your lover take your preferences into account? Or does he continue to treat you generically (all women want "hearts and flowers" all the time, all men want sex all the time)? If your lover continues to treat you generically, it's time to ask yourself what the relationship is about.

WARNING SIGN #2

POSSESSIVENESS

FIVE

You Belong to Me

THE TOGETHERNESS SYNDROME

All Mine

Mary looked drawn and tired today. She apologized for yawning, saying she had slept poorly the night before. "The nightmares keep me up," she explained, "I see him coming at me, that look on his face . . ." I nodded. Victims of domestic violence frequently suffer from posttraumatic stress disorder, a common symptom of which are recurring distressing dreams of the event. We talked for a while about her nightmares, and then I said, "Let's keep unraveling how this all came about, Mary. Let's go back to the early times. Once it was established that you and John were in a relationship, what was it like? How did he behave toward you?"

Mary sat for a moment, thinking, then she said, "When I was a kid, there was this couple down the block, they were about 20–22 years old, maybe, but to me, age 11, they seemed so worldly and mature. They were always together, heads close, whispering, laughing, talking soft, as if they shared some marvelous secret that no one else could ever get in on. You never saw one without the other. Well, that was the way it was with John and me. From the first time we slept together, we were together. He'd drop by my work, we'd go for lunch or just a quick coffee. He'd either pick me up from work or be on my doorstep, grinning, with a red rose or a daisy or some silly wonderful little thing he'd picked up on the way. If for some reason we didn't spend the night together, he'd call first thing in the morning, or show up with a doughnut and a smile."

Mary smiled, remembering, "I was so in love! I had never been so desired, so wanted, and not just sexually, he wanted to know my every thought, my every feeling. He was like—hungry—for all of me, all the time."

"I'd planned lunch with a girlfriend one day; well, he got real angry—saying it was time stolen from us, and asked me to cancel it. I wasn't going to," Mary said, looking at me, "I mean I am my own person, Dr. Noelle, but," Mary said as she continued her story, "he started making love to me and telling me how beautiful I was and how he loved me so and how he wanted me all for himself. I couldn't resist, I called my friend and canceled. And before I knew it, I wasn't seeing any of my friends anymore— just him." Mary's voice became very soft, very tender as she went on, "Only he was so wonderful, always wanting to be so close, tender and intimate, I didn't care. He would hold me tight and put his hands on my face, his fingers caressing my eyes and say "Mine, all mine," and his fingers would trail to my lips and he'd kiss them saying "Mine, all mine," and down to my heart, "Mine, all mine." He would almost croon—he would be so loving, I was like putty in his hands."

Jealousy Prevails

"You know, I've been thinking about what you asked last time, Dr. Noelle," said Bob, as he came in for a session, "I've been thinking about it a lot." Bob seemed agitated. I had no idea what he was talking about. "Refresh my memory, Bob," I said. "We talked about a lot of things." "Yeah," he said, "but it's that thing you asked me on the way out, about was Karen possessive and did she tend to want to be with me all the time in the beginning?" Now I remembered, thankfully. "Oh, yes," I said, "and you said 'No, not particularly,' that she very much had a life of her own."

"Yeah, well, that's not quite right," Bob replied. "I mean Karen did have a life of her own, and she didn't want to be with me all the time. But what I figured out when I thought about it, Doc, was that Karen wanted to be with me whenever *she* wanted to be with me—regardless of what I was up to or wanted. Karen expected me to drop everything when she called. And that's possessive, right?" Bob asked, looking at me for confirmation. "Yes Bob," I said, "it is. Karen was treating you like a possession, like something that belonged to her, that she had a right to control." Bob nodded: "I see it now. I just never thought about it that way before. Of course, the way Karen was, whenever she whistled, I ran. I'd never had such passion in my life, and I sure wasn't going to let such a good thing go by."

Bob stopped for a moment, rubbed his face with his hands, took a breath. He seemed calmer as he continued: "She was possessive in other ways too. There was never any question of my seeing another woman. Karen made it very clear that if she ever found me with someone else, she'd kill me, and claw the other woman's eyes out." Bob smiled ruefully, "It sounded hokey and dramatic, but I didn't care. I loved it."

"So Karen was jealous," I said. "Jealous!" Bob exclaimed. "That's an understatement. Karen wouldn't even let me see my ex-wife! I have a couple of kids, boy and a girl. I would see them every other weekend, you know, the usual. Well, once Karen came into my life, that whole thing changed. She would get really angry any time my ex-wife wanted something for the kids, and I started to see my ex-wife in a whole other light! I'd never thought about how much she was taking me for, but Karen made it very clear that my ex-wife was just out to milk me for all I was worth. I felt Karen was really on my side, protecting me from being too much of a Mister Nice Guy. That felt great. I really appreciated it.

"Karen would always come with me when I picked up the kids—to protect me, she'd say, from my ex, and I was fine with that—except the kids were funny about it. They'd complain they never had private time with me anymore, whining, 'Why does she always have to come along?' Karen pointed out to me how selfish they were; they didn't want to see me happy. I hadn't realized until Karen pointed it out what selfish brats they'd turned into. Their mother's fault, Karen was quick to explain; what could you expect from a woman who got everything for free?

"So I didn't see the kids as much. I hardly realized it at the time, it just seemed like Karen would have something else really urgent she wanted to do a lot of the time on my kids' weekends, and the kids, well, they didn't seem to mind."

Bob was quiet for a moment, then said ruefully, "At least not that I knew of at the time."

Just You and Me

Peter's bruises were healing well, although he still held his head somewhat stiffly, as if afraid to move too quickly. He was also feeling better. "I'm less depressed,"

Peter said, and then added half jokingly, "I don't feel that my life is totally over." I smiled, "Good—that's an improvement. Are you willing for us to keep sorting out how this all happened?" Peter stared into space for a moment, then turned to me with resolve, "Sure, I'm ready. What do you want to know?" I asked Peter if there was anything that bothered him about how Tony behaved toward him in the *beginning*, once he and Tony were actually in a relationship.

"Huh," Peter said, thinking my question over. "I suppose when I think about it now, Tony was pretty pushy," he said, "only I didn't think about it then. All I did was stand there amazed at this incredible love energy that was whirling into my life. I mean Tony was just that, amazing. I don't know if that man ever slept; he had energy enough for three people. After the picnic night, he pretty much installed himself at my place. I mean, he never formally moved in; he just would leave something of his each time he was over, which was all the time. So we never talked about it, it just— was." Peter stopped. In the silence I asked, "Was Tony ever possessive or jealous?"

Peter thought for a moment, then said, "We'd go out to the clubs together, and he'd always stand real close. He'd be whispering wild and sexy comments in my ear about the other guys there, telling me which ones were hot for me and teasing me about it, and then telling me if I went near another guy, I was dead meat. It was so thrilling! I never had a romance like this. It was deliciously intense.

"I loved that part of his jealousy. But he could be a pest about other things. If God forbid the phone rang at the house, and he picked it up first, he'd say 'Peter's not here; I'm his lover, I'll take a message,' when I'd be standing not ten feet away. The first few times I confronted him with 'What's this all about?' he'd just brush me aside with 'You don't need them, you've got me. Besides, it wasn't important.' He'd follow it up with something silly and romantic like turn the radio up real loud and say 'Wanna dance?' He'd sweep me in his arms and do these sexy tango steps, and I'd be mesmerized, bewitched, enchanted. Or he'd yell out 'Pizza time!' and grab his jacket and be halfway out the door before he'd turn back and say 'Coming?' with this huge grin at me. What was I to do? He was positively irresistible.

"Of course if the phone rang and I picked it up first, he would make it soooo uncomfortable to talk. He'd find a million reasons why I had to get off the phone right now, and boy was he creative! My favorite is when he yelled out 'The toilet's overflowing, help!' and I slammed the phone down, ran into the bathroom, only to find him calmly sitting on the edge of the tub, in a perfectly dry bathroom. I started to get pissed, but he just laughed and said, 'Now I know how much you really love me,' dropped to his knees and proceeded to make love to me right there right then. I was helpless in the face of such passion.

"If a friend dropped by, he'd stay right by my side, sitting very close, usually touching me or petting me the whole time. He wouldn't say anything really, he just somehow made it clear that the friend was dropping in on a very private and very intimate situation—and friends just stopped coming by."

Peter sat silently, remembering. "Before long, there was just him and me," he continued, "I really didn't see anyone else any more, and friends stopped calling. The funniest part is, I hardly noticed. I'd never known such devotion. He was so wrapped up in me that he took the place of everybody—and it was perfectly fine by me."

Ms. Know It All

Teri seemed less anxious when she walked in for our third session. She smiled as she sat down, "Well, now I know one way these talks are helping—I didn't have a nightmare last night or the night before." "That's good," I said, "I'm glad. You'll probably still have nightmares for a while, but they should come less often, and eventually hardly ever." "Good," Teri said, "that's a relief. So what do you want us to talk about today?" I smiled. It seemed like Teri was starting to behave more like the person she had described herself as being prior to her experience with Anne. "Well," I replied, "I'd like to know how Anne behaved toward you once the two of you were rooming together, and if there was anything that bothered you about how she behaved toward you at that time. Let's take it from there." "OK," Teri said. She chewed her lower lip pensively for a moment. "Anne was very generous with me," Teri said. "She was always lending me clothes, telling me 'No, don't wear that, you'll look so much better in this,' and she was right. She had great taste. And she'd tell me how to style my hair and redid my makeup for me. It was just so nice. I loved all the attention. It felt great for someone to really care about me, about how I looked and felt and all. And she would move the furniture around, I'd come home from work and presto—the whole living room would be different! It was great fun, I never knew what to expect."

"You enjoyed the spontaneity," I commented. "Yes, I did—except," Teri said, grimacing, "I don't think she liked my things much. Little by little they seemed to end up in storage a lot. And if I wanted to wear something different from what she thought I should wear, she'd get real funny about it. She'd say things like I didn't appreciate how much she wanted me to look my best and stuff like that. So I'd usually end up wearing whatever it was she thought would be best, and she'd brighten right up."

Teri shifted positions on the couch and took a sip of water. She continued: "Anne taught me all the right places to go, clubs and museums and like that, and what movies I should see, with her, of course. I thought it was great. She was real sophisticated, and I was only too happy to have her show me the ropes. Only she really got pissy if I wanted to go do something on my own, so I didn't mostly. And if I met someone and introduced her, she'd be real sweet in front of the person, but then afterwards, when they were gone, she'd point out to me all the reasons why this person wasn't really a good person for me to be around. Well you know, she made me think a lot, she being older than me and knowing more about the world. And as long as we did things her way, she was such a joy to be with, heck, I didn't care." Teri stopped in her recitation. "I guess I should have cared, huh, Dr. Noelle." She hung her head and her voice quavered with sadness, "I feel so stupid." "You're not stupid, Teri," I said gently, "you just didn't see things for what they were. How could you? You didn't know what to look for, what Anne's behavior meant. And you got hurt." "Yeah, I did. I really got hurt," Teri said, and then she cried.

Case Analysis

The picture that most often comes to mind when people think of possessiveness and jealousy is a dramatic scene of a husband or wife yelling at his or her partner for paying attention to some other man or woman, or slapping or hitting the partner for just looking at someone else. Possessiveness and jealousy, however, don't start out like that. In the beginning phases of a violent domestic relationship, possessiveness and jealousy start out looking like the intense involvement typical of the "honeymoon" phase of any close relationship, platonic or romantic. Because of this, possessiveness and jealousy are not often seen as the precursors to abusive behavior until violence sets in later in the relationship.

"I WANT POWER OVER AND CONTROL OF YOU"

It feels great to be special to someone, to have someone want to be with you, just you, someone who thinks your words, your presence, your laughter are the most wonderful in the world. How many songs, books, and movies have been devoted to the yearning for someone who will think you're "it," the center of the universe, at least of that person's universe. And finally there you are, in a relationship with someone who cares, really cares about you, cares so much in fact, that he wants you all to himself—what could be better? A relationship where the caring didn't involve wanting you all to himself would be better—much better.

When abusers want you all for themselves, they are not caring about you. They are caring about themselves: what you can do for them, how you make them feel. A genuine relationship involves mutual caring: caring about yourself and what the other can do for you *and* caring about your partner and what you can do for him or her. The problem with violent domestic relationships is that abusers don't see their partners as individuals, with their own identity, rights, desires, hopes, and dreams. Abusers see their partners as possessions, things that belong to them and exist for the sole purpose of pleasing them. Placed in this context, it's much easier to understand why abusers behave as they do.

When you buy a pair of shoes, you probably put a lot of thought into the kind of shoes you want to get and what you want them to look and feel like. You may then expend considerable energy finding just the right pair of shoes. But once you've bought them, you expect to be able to do whatever you want with those shoes: wear them, not wear them, arrange them neatly in the closet, throw them anywhere in the room, polish them, not polish them, whatever. You don't concern yourself with what the shoes want—that would seem ridiculous to you. You have absolute power over and control of your shoes. This feels right and natural to you.

Well, it feels just as right and natural to abusers to have absolute power over and control of their partner. As far as abusers are concerned, that partner is bought and paid for, bought with attention and paid for with affection. The abuser owns the partner. Abusers experience ownership as giving them power over their partner, which is the *right* to run their life, and control of the partner, which is *how* abusers carry out that right.

Abusers will justify their right to run your life on the basis of their love and caring for you. This sounds great to many people: "Hey, here's somebody who cares so much about my well-being that he or she is trying to steer me on the right course, make sure I get what's best for me." But the hidden implication is demeaning: You don't know what's best for you, you don't know how to run your own life, and the abuser does. Eventually such hidden implications become overt statements that erode your self-esteem.

Abusers don't just give feedback or opinions on how they think their partner ought to run his or her life, they actively control what the partner does. This is what differentiates a genuine relationship from one based on power and control. Friends, for example, feel perfectly entitled to give you their opinion on how you're running your life, but do not feel entitled to then insist that you act according to their opinions. Abusers do. The longer the relationship goes on, the more control abusers will exercise and the more areas of their partner's life such control will encompass.

Right from the beginning of a violent domestic relationship, abusers will typically seek to control your time, who you see, and how often. To a lesser degree, abusers will also attempt at this stage of the relationship to control what you wear, where you go, what you do, what you say, and to whom.

"YOUR TIME BELONGS TO ME"

Always Together

From the first time they made love, Mary and John were together. Not only would Mary and John spend most nights, evenings, and weekends together, but John would also drop by Mary's workplace unexpectedly, picking her up for lunch or coffee. If he wasn't waiting for her at her workplace at the end of the day, he was at her doorstep by the time she got home. To Mary, John's unexpected visits and the amount of time they spent together were wonderfully romantic. She cherished John's constant attention. Mary failed to notice how controlling John's behavior was. By showing up whenever he knew Mary would have a free moment, John ensured that Mary spent all her free time with him.

As soon as Mary made plans to spend time with someone else, John insisted she cancel those plans, saying it was time "stolen" from the two of them.

"I was very much in love with John," said Mary, "I prized our time together as much as he did. That's why I was so surprised when he objected to my seeing my girlfriend for lunch. I wasn't taking time away from us. At least I didn't think I was. I thought of lunch time as, well, my time. You know, time to do errands, or talk on the phone, just a break in the day. But John made it real clear that all my time was 'us' time. I didn't want to hurt his feelings, and he was so persuasive." Mary went along with John's desire, until finally she wasn't seeing any of her friends anymore. John now had complete control of Mary's time.

"Wow," you say to yourself, "that Mary is spineless. I'd never do that. I'd see my friends no matter what!" Maybe. But my experience tells me otherwise. Most of us, finding ourselves in a relationship where we are made to feel so special, will do anything to preserve that relationship. Suddenly everything and everyone else seems secondary, and you do, all too often, become willing to give your partner whatever he wants, in this case, all your time.

Your time, of course, is what makes up your life. The time you share with your partner is never again available to you to spend elsewhere. When abusers insist on controlling their partner's time, they are controlling their partner's life.

Constant Availability

Karen's way of controlling Bob's time was different. She did not control Bob's time by being with him all the time, but rather by insisting on his instant availability to her. The outcome is the same. In order to be available to Karen whenever she wanted to see him, Bob couldn't make other plans, or he had to be willing to drop those plans at any moment. His life was not his own.

Privatizing Behavior

Tony's approach to controlling Peter's time was more like John's. He unofficially moved in with Peter and saw to it that they were together all the time. But Tony also controlled Peter's time by privatizing that time. In other words, when friends stopped by, Tony behaved in such a private or intimate manner with Peter that they would go away, feeling they had intruded on a very special moment.

When I asked Peter how he felt about Tony's privatizing behaviors, he said, "Confused. It was really strange. On the one hand I was flattered that he was willing to be really open with how he felt about me. On the other hand, it felt a little creepy, like our intimacy was being putting on show, somehow." Peter stopped for a moment, thinking, then continued, "I didn't know until much later how that kind of behavior pushed my friends away. I had no idea. And when my friends first told me," he said laughing, "I just thought they were jealous. Took a while before I figured out what was really going on."

It usually does take a while. Abusers control your time in such pleasant ways in the beginning that most people either don't realize what's going on or don't find the controlling behavior particularly offensive. Certainly that was the case with Teri.

Bribery

"Control my time? Are you kidding? From the time we moved in together," Teri said, "I was either working or with Anne. I knew it, but I didn't care. I was having a blast! Anne would take me places, she would pay for pretty much everything. It was great!"

Bribery works. As crass as it may sound, we're all susceptible to someone taking us places and showing us a good time. Abusers are well aware of this, and only too willing to "buy" your time as a way of controlling it.

Controlling your time is only the first step in controlling your life. Controlling who you see and under what circumstances is the second.

"I'LL TELL YOU WHO YOU CAN SEE, AND WHEN, AND WHERE"

There is a certain jealousy that accompanies close relationships. You want your mate to be primarily interested in you. For example, you have a pang of jealousy when your mate talks at length with an interesting man or woman at the company picnic, even if there isn't any obvious flirtation going on. You want your best friend to be *your* best friend; you feel a pang of jealousy when she tells you about a particularly wonderful encounter with another friend. These feelings are normal. They come from our fear of loss, the fear we all have of losing those people and things that have become precious to us. That fear is usually proportionate to the reality of the threat. You are more fearful of losing your mate to a fascinating sexually attractive unattached individual of little scruples who is decidedly "on the make," for example, than you are of losing your mate to a jogging buddy.

Abusers do not discriminate well between differing levels of threat. To abusers, anyone and everyone is a threat and represents a potential enemy.

Excluding Friends

Mary's girlfriends represented no real threat to John. "None of my girlfriends were 'swingers'," Mary told me. "We were all a pretty straight bunch; it wasn't like I wanted to escape to an all-night disco or something and party—all I wanted to do was see my friends occasionally for lunch. But that didn't seem to matter," Mary said, sighing. "Did John have an opportunity to meet your friends and find that out for himself?" I asked. "Oh," Mary said, "he didn't want to meet them. He said he didn't care how wonderful they were, he just didn't want anyone taking me away from him. It sounded great at the time, so romantic," Mary continued, "he certainly was up front about it."

By excluding her friends, John tied Mary more tightly to himself. He also accomplished another equally important goal: ensuring that Mary would not be susceptible to her friends' possibly negative opinion of him.

Abusers seek to exclude others from your life, not only because they fear that those others will take you from them literally, but also because they fear the influence of others on you. If you don't see your friends or family on a regular basis, and if you abandon your social life at the request of your partner, your friends and family can't give you feedback and reflection on your life. They can't provide the outside validation and reality checks so valuable to each of us. They are not there to steer you away from a potentially dangerous partner.

Abusers want to be the most important person in your life, preferably the only person. They want you to be available to them just as your shoe is available to you, that is to say, all the time. Abusers systematically exclude not only anyone they perceive as a direct threat, but also anyone or anything that might make you less available to them, for example, in Bob's case, his children.

Excluding Family

Karen had no apparent interest in Bob's children or in supporting Bob's role as a parent. She was quick to criticize the children's behavior and point out how their mother was responsible for their brattiness, but offered nothing in the way of helpful ideas or solutions. She actively discouraged Bob from seeing his children, making her needs and wants more important than theirs.

"I had no idea what it was doing to my children," Bob said, "I feel worse about that now than about anything else. I abandoned my kids. Oh, not technically, I sent child support and saw them occasionally, but I stopped seeing them as regularly, I stopped being as involved as I had been in their day-to-day activities and interests. I stopped being there for them in the way they were used to, in the way I had been. I was there for Karen." "But you didn't see that at the time," I said. "No," Bob replied, "Karen made everything about her so important, supporting her, being there for her, doing for her, that it took up all my energy, all my focus." "Did your kids say anything about it to you?" I asked. "Well, in the beginning they asked why Karen always had to come along. I thought it was just normal kid jealousy of me being serious about a woman that wasn't their Mom," Bob explained, "and when they asked for time alone with me, I bought what Karen said, that it was just them whining. And after a while, they stopped asking, and I thought everything was OK again. It's only after the divorce I found out my children had just given up," Bob's voice faltered, "given up on me." Bob had made himself completely available to Karen, at the expense of his relationship with his children.

Just the Two of Us

Sexual availability and exclusivity are important areas of control to abusers. Tony excluded other sexual encounters from Peter's life by always being with him when encounters were likely, such as at gay bars and clubs, and by making clear and direct threats. Such threats generally sound romantic and thrilling to the person receiving them, romantic and thrilling, that is, until the abusers actually live up to their words, as Tony did later on.

Tony didn't just limit his exclusion to potential sexual partners, he sought to exclude from Peter's life anyone and everyone who might want some of Peter's attention or affection. Tony was very direct, telling Peter that he didn't need other people. "You've got me," he would say. Tony made it impossible for Peter to maintain any kind of communication with friends by failing to deliver telephone messages and getting Peter off the telephone if he happened to be engaged in conversation.

By Her Side

Anne also sought to control who Teri saw and when. She discouraged Teri from going out on her own, which would have opened the door to Teri meeting other friends. Anne also saw to it that she organized all their outings, keeping Teri close by her side. In so doing, she not only controlled who Teri saw, but also what Teri did.

"I'LL PICK YOUR CLOTHES, YOUR HAIRSTYLE, YOUR EVERYTHING"

In addition, Anne exercised a different kind of control over Teri. Anne dictated how Teri dressed, styled her hair, and applied her makeup, by lending Teri clothes, helping Teri style her hair, and giving her makeup hints. Such generosity becomes control when it ceases to take into account how the receiver feels about the gift. "Did you like the way Anne suggested you dress and do your hair?" I asked Teri. "Sometimes, yes," Teri replied, "but a lot of the time it didn't real feel like me, you know?" I nodded. "Only Anne didn't care about that," Teri continued. "How I felt about it didn't seem to matter. Anne would tell me I didn't know what looked good on me, and at the time I thought maybe she was right. I mean, she was the sophisticated one." Anne gave Teri grooming help and advice, not for Teri's greater good, which would have taken into account Teri's tastes and preferences, but as ways to control her. Little girls dress up their dolls without asking the doll's feelings about it; "She's my dolly," they say. Teri became Anne's "dolly."

Anne moved furniture around and packed Teri's off into storage without consulting Teri. Anne showed the same disregard for Teri's rights in moving her furniture as she had in breaking Teri's lease. Anne assumed, as you do of a possession, that she was free to do whatever she wanted with Teri's life.

HOW YOU ARE MANIPULATED AND CONTROLLED

An abuser does not relate to his or her partner as an equal. In an abusive relationship, you are always in one of two positions: on the pedestal or off the pedestal. While you are on the pedestal, all is well and good, and abusers will make every effort to please and appease you. When you are off the pedestal, the abuser feels entitled to treat you contemptuously. Neither position contributes to the health of a relationship. Since abusers do not treat their partners as equals, they do not consult or negotiate with them. Abusers seek to satisfy their wants and needs either by using overt control, when the passive partner is off the pedestal, or by manipulation, when the passive partner is on the pedestal.

Manipulation is a covert way of controlling people. Abusers use manipulation most frequently in the beginning stages of the relationship, when you're on the pedestal. Overt control, which includes threats, demands, pushing, shoving, and hitting, is the way abusers control their partners after the "honeymoon" phase of the relationship, when you are off the pedestal. In learning to recognize the warning signs of a violent domestic relationship, it is very helpful to pay attention to how someone is trying to affect your behavior. The four relationships we've been exploring illustrate some of the most common manipulative approaches.

Romantic or Sexual Seduction

This is John's primary manipulative strategy. He gets Mary to stop seeing her friends by invoking the romantic "us," as in "takes away from time for 'us'," and reinforces that romantic message by sexually seducing her. During his sexual seduction, he incorporates many romantic messages, such as reiterating to Mary his love for her, how he wants her all to himself, how beautiful she is, staying very close to her, and being very intimate.

Romantic ideals of closeness, togetherness, and belonging are powerful in our society. Thousands upon thousands of romance novels, billboards, magazines, and advertisements reinforce the romantic ideal. "I really felt like I was living a romance novel," Mary said. "Me! It was incredible, I was literally swept off my feet." The reality of what living such an ideal might mean is easily forgotten in the heady rush of passion. "I wasn't paying any attention to what it really meant for me to be giving up my friends so easily," Mary continued, "I was busy living the most unbelievable romance of my life, and I just didn't want it to stop."

Logic and Reason

Although Karen certainly used sexual seduction to manipulate Bob, she also used, with great effectiveness, a common although rarely recognized manipulation—

manipulation through reason. This manipulation uses the "for your own good" or "for the good of the relationship" approach.

This approach is particularly difficult for passive partners to see because it doesn't seem like manipulation. It just seems like someone appealing to your rational mind, helping you see something that you should have realized was good for you (and the relationship) in the first place.

"I'm on Your Side"

To control the amount of time and attention Bob gave to his children, Karen began her manipulation by apparently siding with Bob. She attacked Bob's ex-wife for taking too much of Bob's money. Karen said she would come along with Bob to pick up the kids because, as she put it:"You're too much of a pushover for her [Bob's ex-wife]. Anytime she says its 'for the kids' you're such a nice guy, you just give her what she wants." When I asked Bob how he felt about that, he said, "On top of the world! I was delighted that Karen saw me as a nice guy. Plus she was right. In a lot of ways I was a pushover when it came to the kids. It felt great to have someone on my side, for a change, protecting my interests."

What Bob didn't notice at the time is how Karen changed the nature of the relationship with his kids. Bob no longer saw his children by himself; Karen was always there too. No matter how nice Karen might have been during these family gatherings, by her very presence, the nature of the father–children interactions changed. When Bob's children complained, Karen redefined the children's understandable request for private time with their Dad into "selfishness." She did so by appealing to Bob's rational mind, giving him all sorts of "for your own good" reasons: "The kids will appreciate you more, you're too nice, I'm trying to help you here." "I loved hearing this stuff, Dr. Noelle," Bob said. "I'm ashamed to admit it, but I bought what Karen was saying hook, line, and sinker."

The Abuser's Needs Come First

Having succeeded in appealing to his rational mind, Karen then got more direct in how she excluded Bob's children from his life. She insisted that her needs come before his parental duties and desires, generally by inventing some pressing matter on his weekend with the kids that Bob had to help her with. "She'd want me to fix something on her car, or help her with some project or other. I'd tell her this was the kids' time and I couldn't, but she'd change my mind somehow," Bob said. "How, Bob?" I challenged. "You're a grown man, you know what you want." "Yeah," Bob said, shaking his head, "but you didn't know Karen. She'd sigh, and say something like 'what a shame you can't see how those children are taking advantage of you' and I'd try to argue back, but she'd just keep at it, showing me all the ways the kids were being unreasonable, and too demanding of my life. By the time she was done, I was convinced!" Bob stopped for a moment, then said, "Let's face it, Doc, I wanted to be convinced. I knew I wasn't just going to be fixing her car. There was a great big carrot attached to my doing stuff for her, and I knew it." Karen reasoned Bob into what she wanted him to do and then reinforced him with great sex. That's powerful manipulation.

"For Your Own Good"

Anne was also extremely adept at manipulating through reason. Anne's way of controlling who Teri saw or spent time with was based on a "for your own good" approach. Anne convinced Teri that her dislike of Teri's friends was based on worldly wisdom and a greater knowledge of people and that she was protecting Teri from harm—all in Teri's best interests. In her naiveté, Teri went along with Anne's way of thinking; she never realized that Anne was manipulating her for *Anne's* own good.

Charm

Tony relied heavily on seductiveness and charm in getting Peter to go along with what he wanted in the beginning of the relationship. Tony was so effective in manipulating Peter with his seductiveness (both sexual and romantic) and his own humorous brand of charm that Peter was literally dazzled by what was going on. "I knew at the time I was letting him get away with some real inappropriate stuff," said Peter, "like telling friends I wasn't available, or never giving me their messages, but he was so outrageous about it, and so off-the-wall funny and adorable, I couldn't hold it against him. By the time he was done being either outrageously charming or outrageously sexy, I'd forgotten what had started it all."

Tony's seductiveness and charm distracted Peter from his inappropriate behavior, much as a magician distracts your attention while pulling a dove from a hat, and every bit as effectively.

Mood Swings

Abusers very deliberately use their moods to control your behavior. In the beginning of a violent domestic relationship, when you please abusers, they reward you with smiles and outpourings of affection or attention. If you displease them, they punish you with whining, grumpiness, griping, and general unpleasantness. This misleads their partners into the kind of thinking common to battered individuals. "If I only could please him/her, everything would be fine." That's not so. The violence abusers inflict on their loved ones explodes from within themselves, the result of a buildup of unexpressed emotions that have little to do with whether you are "pleasing" them. The sad truth is, abusers are just as caught in a cycle of abuse as their victims. At this early stage, however, abusers are much more in charge of themselves and use emotions to manipulate their partners into various behaviors.

Anne, for example, used her mood switches manipulatively. She would be warm and affectionate and generous when Teri was going along with her wishes, but as soon as Teri preferred a different way of doing things, Anne would get "real funny about it" or "pissy." In the interests of keeping things nice, given the overall "wonderfulness" of the friendship at this stage, Teri would go along with Anne. Anne would immediately brighten up or get nice again, having successfully manipulated Teri into the desired behavior.

SIX

How to Stay in Charge
of Your Own Life

POWER AND CONTROL

Abusers seek to own you—heart, body, and soul. Their ultimate goal is to control what you think, what you feel, what you do, how you dress, where you go—everything about you. An abusive individual cannot, however, "own" you unless you allow it. Guard against becoming involved in a potentially violent domestic relationship by staying true to yourself and in charge of your life.

Be Who You Really Are

Be your own person. One of the most difficult things to do when you're in the throes of an intense relationship, sexual or otherwise, is to keep a sense of who you are.

Abusive individuals will want you to be what suits their needs, fantasies, and projections, not who you really are. Don't let yourself get sucked in by their idealized version of who they want you to be. If you enjoy quiet evenings at home and an occasional outing with friends, don't become, for example, a party animal because that's what your new lover is into. If your idea of working out is lifting the remote control, don't turn into a fitness buff who runs every morning at 5 a.m. and does yoga for two hours a night because that's what suits your new significant other. Resist that idealized version, and be yourself.

Certainly, if your new lover opens your eyes to a different way of doing things and you'd like to try that for a while, do so. But be very clear and tell your partner that you are trying this new behavior on for size, and it may or may not fit. If your new lover insists on your changing your ways in a manner that does not agree with what you want, say no, and pay attention to further attempts to control your behavior. True love enhances who you are; it does not take away from who you are. True love does not demand that you be other than whom you freely choose to be.

Love Isn't about Agreement

Continue to do the things you enjoy and espouse the beliefs that are true for you. If you don't agree with a philosophy or moral point of view your friend has, don't be afraid to say so. Passive partners often have a great deal of trouble understanding that love does not mean agreement. People in healthy relationships can agree to disagree on any number of issues without damaging the relationship. Changes you choose to make in your life must be because you decide those changes are the right thing for you, not because you're afraid your friend will abandon you if you don't make those changes.

CONTROLLING YOUR TIME

Ultimately, abusers want you to spend all your time only with them, or, put another way, abusers want your total and complete attention. Even when abusive individuals don't want you around, they expect you in some way to be giving them attention (thinking about them, doing for them) and they don't want you giving your time and attention to anyone else unless it is part of doing something for them.

Giving of Your Time

Controlling your time, then, becomes an issue early on in the relationship. If you find yourself giving more of your time to your new lover or friend than you really want to, ask yourself, "Why am I doing this? Am I sacrificing anything important to me (hobbies, other activities) by giving all this time to this person? Am I giving in to my lover's desire for time because I'm scared he'll leave me otherwise?" Be honest with yourself. Staying aware of what's real for you and making conscious choices will help you steer clear of a potentially unhealthy relationship.

If your new lover or friend objects to your desire to spend your time as you see fit, talk about it. Explain how your hobbies, activities, and other ways you spend your time are important to you. People involved in a healthy relationship are usually able to give each other the space to live their respective lives and yet maintain sufficient togetherness. Does your new lover seem threatened by your involvement in various activities? You are much better off talking about these things than avoiding discussion, as passive partners often do, in order to not "break the mood." Better to break the mood than risk ruining your life! If your partner is unwilling to openly discuss such matters, his possessiveness of your time might be an attempt to control you. Partners in a healthy relationship discuss such matters continually over the life of a relationship as interests and time commitments change.

The "If You Really Loved Me" Trap

Don't fall into the trap of "If you really loved me you'd spend more time with me," or any variations on that theme. Someone who tries to guilt you into spending more time with him isn't being loving, he is being manipulative. As the relationship grows and develops over time, each of your activities and interests will become integrated into the relationship, and your time arrangements will naturally shift and change accordingly. The key word is *time*, not as in more time with the new person, but as in taking the time to see how the various parts of your respective lives shift and change to fit well together. The abusive individual, lacking trust in the natural development of the relationship, will try to force this fit.

CONTROLLING THE PEOPLE YOU SEE AND UNDER WHAT CIRCUMSTANCES

Since abusive individuals want all your attention and affection for themselves, they quickly seek to eliminate any competition for that attention, namely your friends and family.

Maintain Ties with Friends and Family

It is often tempting, in the intensity of the beginnings of a relationship, to devote all of your waking hours to your new lover or friend. As understandable as this is, it is not a good idea. The message you send to your new significant other is that the other people in your life do not matter. You are perfectly willing to sacrifice friends and family for this new relationship. This is music to an abuser's ears. You may be thinking, "Oh well, it doesn't matter, the newness will wear off in a month or two and I'll go back to my normal habits of seeing my friends." That may be so, but in the meantime, you are depriving yourself of a prime way of finding out if your new lover is trying to control you. If so, you need to know it now, not in a couple of months when you may find it difficult to change patterns that have been established in the relationship.

Friends and family are also your most honest source of feedback. You need to stay in touch with those who know you best when you are involved in an intense relationship. They will help provide you with a good counterbalance to your emotional high.

Restricting Interactions with Friends and Family

One of the quickest ways of determining if your lover is trying to control you is to keep seeing your friends and family at about the same frequency as you did before the relationship began. If your lover puts pressure on you to see less of your friends and talk less with them on the telephone, or in any way makes it difficult for you to interact with your friends and family as you would like, pay attention. This person is trying to control you.

Talk with your lover about your need to see friends and family. If your lover simply was caught up in the excitement of a new relationship and was unaware of how it was cutting you off from those who matter to you, he will back off. If, however, your lover continues to try to keep you from friends and family, you are at risk of being involved with an abusive individual.

Don't let the person's like or dislike of your friends and family influence which ones you continue to see. Be true to your own likes and dislikes. Listen to your lover's criticisms and opinions, certainly, but use your own mind and heart to discern what truth those criticisms and opinions may hold. Only make those changes you would make regardless of whether the person stays in your life.

Co-opting Friends and Family

Abusive individuals will sometimes take the opposite tack and seek to co-opt your friends and family. This approach is easily recognizable, because they will insist on accompanying you wherever you go and will do whatever it takes to get your friends and family to look upon them with the same adoring eyes that you currently do. They may be perfectly willing for you to see whomever you wish as long as they are glued to your side. Abusive individuals effectively eliminate all competition for your attention and affection by adding themselves to the mix. Your interaction with friends and family will become about your new lover, not about you and them. You lose the benefit of any accurate feedback from your friends and family, as well as the emotional counterbalance they can provide. As nice as togetherness is, keep your perspective on the relationship by reserving some "by yourself" time with friends and family.

CONTROLLING WHAT YOU WEAR
AND YOUR ENVIRONMENT

If a new friend suggests that you dress a certain way and you enjoy these suggestions, that's great. Make sure, however, that you give yourself plenty of opportunities to find out whether the suggestions of outfits is a demand or really a suggestion. A demand or insistence that you dress a certain way is characteristic of an abusive individual; a suggestion is fun and in no way harmful.

Similarly, if an individual simply rearranges your environment without asking your permission, that's abusive. You're an adult, with the right to your environment however you see fit. If your friend demands or insists on a different environment, that's abusive, just as failing to ask permission to make such changes is abusive. In a healthy relationship, people have opinions on each other's tastes and express preferences, but they don't demand or insist. They suggest, and they honor each other's freedom to go along with a suggestion or ignore it.

Changing Your Life

Beyond being very insistent about your making changes in how you dress and your environment, abusive individuals often ask you to make radical changes in your life, such as move, follow them to a different state, change the nature of your work, or stop working in order to spend more time together. Abusive individuals will put all sorts of conditions on how you must live in order to be with them, such as give up your pets, change your daily routine to accommodate theirs, drive a certain kind of car, and so on.

All of these changes may indeed suit you; however, these are changes that need to be examined very closely when you are at the beginning of a relationship. Much of what abusive individuals are doing in requesting or demanding these changes is seeing how solid their power over and control of you are. The more you are willing to sacrifice, change, or alter in the name of the relationship, the more likely you are to stay in that relationship through thick and thin. Make only those changes that feel absolutely right for you and that you would be very happy with should your new lover walk out on you tomorrow.

MANIPULATION

Manipulation is how abusers own you. It's what they do to make sure you stay owned. Romantic, sexual seduction and charm are high on the list of what abusers do in the beginning stages to keep you under their control. Beatings and battering come later. One of the most effective manipulations is the use of reason, the "I'm showing you this for your own good" approach.

Know Your Likes and Dislikes

The more you know who you really are, the less susceptible you will be to any kind of manipulation. Passive partners often are unsure of the "rightness" of their likes and dislikes, desires and preferences, yet there is no right or wrong in this area, there is only what pleases you and what doesn't. Know your own mind. Know what you like, dislike, believe in, don't believe in; know your values and preferences, know how you want to run your life, and be willing to commit to what works for you.

Be aware of the power of charm and romantic and sexual seduction. Become suspicious if your new lover starts using any one of these to get you to agree to something. Most of us know when we are being manipulated, so use that sense to your advantage. Don't let yourself get romanced or seduced into a behavior, lifestyle, situation, or anything else that is not right for you. That's why it's so important to know your own mind. If you don't, you're easy prey for an abuser.

Accept Only What Works for You

Don't take on a belief, value, or lifestyle just because the new person in your life says it's better for you. Be willing to think and feel for yourself. Certainly it's important to listen to new ideas, to be willing to change, to be flexible and grow, but it's equally important to investigate whatever new thought, belief, or behavior your lover suggests to you before you go for it. Ask yourself how adopting this new thought, belief, or behavior would fit with the rest of your life. Look at the potential consequences and at what other people's experience with such has been. Only adopt new ideas, behaviors, or lifestyles if you would adopt them regardless of whether the new person stays in your life. Then your partner has not manipulated you. Instead, you have freely chosen to incorporate a new idea in your life, which just happened to have been suggested by your lover.

Emotional Blackmail

Mood swings are another way abusive individuals seek to manipulate. If your lover gets angry, let's say, when you don't want to go along with something, such as going to an event, stand your ground. Do nothing. In other words, resist the temptation to "fix it" for her. Don't attempt to make her feel better by giving in and going to the event. Then watch what happens. If she continues to be angry, ask yourself: "Is this how I want to interact in a relationship? Do I want to be involved with someone who can't take no for an answer?"

In a healthy relationship, lovers or friends might be disappointed if you didn't want to accompany them to an event they wanted to attend, but once you had made it clear that you really didn't want to go, they would make other arrangements. They would not try to get you to go by blackmailing you with an unpleasant emotion. Don't run your life according to whether your choices will put your lover or friend in a good mood or a bad mood. Run your life as you see fit, taking your partner into account, but not making your partner's mood the primary determinant of what you do.

WARNING SIGN #3

The Switch

SEVEN

Dr. Jekyll Becomes Mr./Ms. Hyde

THE DARK SIDE EMERGES

It was unseasonably warm, even for California. Mary came in wearing shorts and a loose top. "I hope you don't mind my wearing shorts," Mary said, "it's just too hot for anything else." I laughed, "Whatever you want to wear is fine, Mary; the fashion police rarely knock on therapists' doors." Mary smiled, "You don't know how good it feels not to worry all the time about what will upset people." "I don't know quite what you mean, Mary," I said, encouraging her to say more on the subject. "I miss him, you know," Mary sighed. "I'm sure you do, Mary; John was a big part of your life," I replied. Mary nodded, "But what I don't miss, Dr. Noelle, is the way he would get so incredibly upset over things, little things, like if I wore shorts when he didn't think I should, or didn't wear them when he thought I should." Mary shook her head, remembering.

"I used to make myself crazy trying to figure out what would set him off." I nodded; I had heard this same statement from so many other partners of abusive individuals. "Mary," I said, "do you remember the first time John got upset in the way you're describing?" Mary thought about it for a moment, then said, "I do, I surely do. It was about three months after we were pretty much living together. I remember I got off work early, so I could get home before John did." Mary smiled at her recollection. "I was real excited and happy because I wanted to fix a special romantic dinner for us. He really liked it when I'd do that. I'd bought candles and wine, his favorite cut of meat, the whole nine yards. Usually he'd greet me with a kiss and a great big hug, saying 'How's my girl?' This time when he came in, he just walked in the door, took one look at the table set all nice, with the candles lit and everything, and he said 'Oh, great' in this 'like I really need this' tone of voice, went straight to the CD player, and put some real whiny depressing music on, very loud. He'd hardly even glanced at me, much less said hello or anything."

Mary shook her head. "I was in shock, Dr. Noelle. I figured something had happened, something awful, and so I went over the couch where he'd plopped himself down and said, 'Honey, what's wrong? Are you OK?' He said 'Not now, Mary, OK?' in a totally disgusted tone of voice. I was so hurt! I didn't know what had happened or if I'd done something wrong, or what. But that was some dismal evening, I can tell you that. John just sat there, playing depressing music, sitting mostly in the dark. He wouldn't talk, look at me, anything. He didn't want dinner, but at some point he grabbed the wine bottle off the table and poured himself a drink. He seemed to be sitting on his anger like a hen guards her eggs. I didn't know what to do, I'd never seen him that way. I cried myself to sleep.

"John didn't come to bed that night. The next morning I got up real early. I really hadn't slept more than a couple of hours on and off. There he was, snoring away, still on the couch. I made him a cup of his favorite coffee, and came over to wake him up, real gently. I knew he had to get to work and I didn't want him to be late. He opened one eye, peered up at me and said, again in that disgusted tone of voice, 'What do you want? Can't you leave me alone, even for just a minute?' I was so upset, Dr. Noelle!" Mary said. "He'd never spoken to me like that, I couldn't believe this was the same man who'd been adoring me for the past three months. Fine, I thought, be late for work, see if I care, and I just got dressed and left.

"When I came home that night, John was still there, on the couch. The house was all dark except for the light from the TV, which was glowing with the picture on and the volume off, the depressing music was on full blast, and he'd progressed from wine to scotch. He didn't say a word to me when I came in. I don't know if he made it to work or not. All I know is this went on for three days. I felt like I was dying. What had happened to my beautiful romance? Anything I tried to do seemed to only make John angrier and more depressed. He was sullen, sulking, as if sitting on a huge mountain of rage.

"On the fourth day, I couldn't stand it any more. It was like living in a dark dank hole with gray water dripping off the walls. I cried and begged and pleaded for him to tell me what was wrong. Finally he said resentfully, 'You hung up on me.' 'What?' I said; I couldn't remember ever doing such a thing. He thrust his face two inches from mine and repeated, angrily through gritted teeth, 'You hung up on me.' 'I did?' I said, surprised. 'You think I lie?' he exploded. 'No!' I exclaimed, frightened by the strength of his reaction. 'Of course not, I just am not remembering it right now.' He laughed bitterly, 'Yeah, right. All you ever remember is what you want to remember. You never think of me.'

"I didn't know what to say, Dr. Noelle. That was so untrue! Plus I couldn't for the life of me remember hanging up on him. I apologized profusely for ever hanging up on him. I didn't dare to say at this point I didn't think I had. And then bit by bit he came out with what was bothering him."

Mary got up and started pacing as she continued her story. "Apparently, that Monday, when he'd called at the office, I had a call come in on 'call waiting' while he and I were chatting on the phone. I asked him to hold the line a moment while I dealt with that call. And somewhere in that transaction, he had gotten cut off. I'd called him right back, and he'd sounded perfectly normal and fine about it. Now he was telling me that once he'd gotten off the phone with me, he'd started thinking about it. He realized he felt horribly rejected, that I would deal with another call while he was on the line. He said that I'd ruined his day, he'd been late to work and messed up because of my inconsiderateness. He finished by saying that I was just a selfish bitch and I was lucky he was still talking to me.

"I was dumbfounded. I didn't know what to make of all this. Was I selfish? Was it really bad of me to have handled that other call? I hated that I was responsible for his being so upset. I felt terrible about it. I apologized and apologized and apologized. I did whatever I could think of to make him feel better and soothe his hurt feelings."

Mary sat back down on the couch as she continued, "Unfortunately, that was only the first of what became many incidents. We'd be going along fine, then suddenly I would 'do' something, something I never would have expected would be hurtful, like wanting to finish dinner in time to go to a show, and John would get upset. That's a prime example." "Of what, Mary?" I asked, encouraging her to continue.

"Of what would make John upset," Mary replied. "Ordinarily John couldn't care less about hanging around at the table once dinner had been eaten. So I thought nothing of it when I asked if we could eat dessert later, so we could get to the show on time. I fully expected John to say 'Sure, let's go.' What I got instead was 'Everything is more important than me, I mean nothing to you. Going to the show is more important to you than me, you know I want to take the time I want over dinner.' Boy, my head was spinning. How could I have guessed that? Usually John was first one up from the table to go over to the television. This kind of thing drove me crazy, Dr. Noelle. My heart would just sink. I knew from his tone that I'd be in for a week of misery."

"Did you talk to John about how you felt?" I asked. "I tried to," Mary replied, "I tried to talk to John about how difficult it was for me when he'd go into one of these upset depressed periods. He'd just throw it back in my face saying how did I expect him to behave when I'd been so rejecting of him. He'd reiterate how horribly I'd hurt him, and how he couldn't help responding in that way. He said all I had to do to change things was to stop hurting him. He didn't seem to realize or care how much his behavior hurt me. There was no talking with him about it, Dr. Noelle, no matter how I tried. It was a closed subject."

THE SCREAMING BEGINS

When I asked Bob when things started to go wrong between himself and Karen, he sighed and said, "Pretty early on, actually." "Are you willing to talk about it?" I asked. "Sure," Bob said, "why not? I hate talking about it, but it does make me feel better when I do." "Sort of like castor oil?" I asked, joking. "Yeah," Bob grinned, "a lot like castor oil. OK. Here goes.

"We'd been seeing each other for—oh, I don't know, something like three—four months. I remember we were standing in line at CostPlus, WalMart, one of those. We were joking and laughing, Karen was flirting with me. We were having a good time. And suddenly she catches one of the cashier helpers staring at her, a young kid, 17 or 18 years old, something like that. She snaps out at him, 'What are you staring at?,' and the kid turns away, kind of embarrassed. Well I said, trying to make her feel better, 'It's nothing, honey, he doesn't mean anything by it,' and suddenly Karen starts in with 'Why do we have to wait in line like this, this is ridiculous, what's wrong with these people, I can't believe I'm being treated this way,' at the top of her lungs, she's so angry!

"I'm dumbfounded. I don't know what to do. I've never seen her behave like this, I try to get her to calm down, telling her it'll be OK, we'll be out of there in no time. She turns on me, screaming, 'How dare you not support me! How dare you tell me to calm down, calm down when I have every right to be angry, whose side are you on?!' and she storms out of the store, leaving me with a shopping cart full of stuff."

Bob shook his head, then continued. "I get through the line as quickly as I can, pay for everything, and as I leave, there she is, pacing away right outside the store. Karen's fuming, we start walking together towards my car. I say something like 'Are you OK, honey?' and she lashes out at me, 'No, I am not OK. I cannot believe how you just stood there and let those people treat me like that and didn't support me.' 'But honey,' I said, 'they weren't doing anything, we were just standing on line . . .' She cut me off, 'Weren't doing anything?! I cannot believe you, I cannot believe you. That boy was looking at me in a dirty way. You saw it and you didn't do anything about it, you . . .' and she got so mad, she kicked the tires on my car.

"I didn't know what to do, so I just tried to take her in my arms. It was like trying to hold a squawking bird, and I kept saying, 'I love you, it's all right, I love you, I won't let anything bad happen to you,' even though I could not understand what she was so upset about. Finally she started crying and then started kissing me real passionately. I was so confused."

Bob stopped for a moment, then addressed me directly, "Karen would do that, Doc. Things would be going great and then suddenly something would set her off. I never knew what it was going to be. It could be something like the kid looking at her, or my saying I thought our appointment with the tax accountant was at 10 a.m. when she thought it was at 11 a.m. or my forgetting to say 'I love you' at the end of a phone conversation. It seemed like anything and everything could trigger it. The only element I finally figured out was common to her outbursts was they were times when she felt I had somehow let her down. That I wasn't there for her when she expected me to be. The problem was, I had no way of knowing what those expectations were, when I was supposed to be there for her.

"I would make every effort to be there for her in those situations that made sense to me, like being there for her when she lost her job, or helping put on a party, or taking care of things when she was sick or tired. But I couldn't even begin to figure out the ones she'd blow up on. My desire to see a different movie from the one she wanted to watch, my asking if she would mind picking her clothes up from the bedroom floor before we went to bed at night, my mentioning once that it would be nice for us to cook a real meal together for a change rather than always pop a frozen dinner in the microwave. All these led to huge outbursts, with Karen ranting and raving about how inconsiderate I was and how dare I be so unsupportive of her and her needs, and how could I let her down and not be there for her. I gave up. I became extraordinarily good at apologizing for things I didn't think I'd done, just in the interests of peace." Bob shook his head, remembering.

"And Karen never let me forget anything, Doc," Bob continued. "Right up until the time we separated, she would bring up that incident with the kid in the store, along with a host of other times I'd 'failed' to be there for her. Whenever I did something she didn't like, she start in on me with one or another of my—by now famous— unsupportive times. She'd go through the whole thing all over again, often working herself up to the same emotional fever she'd been in whenever the event happened. It was amazing to me that she could keep that much emotion alive on such incidents."

"Did you let Karen know how you felt about all this?" I asked. "I'd try to talk to her about how confusing it was for me, and how hurtful when she would say I wasn't there for her, wasn't supportive of her," Bob answered, "but it was like talking to a brick wall. She'd just look at me like I was crazy and say, What did I expect? How was she supposed to behave when I was betraying her like that? I wouldn't know what to say. I wouldn't even realize until I thought about it later that it all got turned back to her somehow."

Bob stopped for a moment, then said, "She never considered my feelings, Doc, how hurtful and difficult her outbursts were for me; it was as if those didn't matter. The only feelings that mattered were hers."

A HURTFUL DISTANCING

Peter considered my question for a moment, then said, "Sure, I remember when things started to go bad with Tony. I remember it very specifically. I was laughing at a TV show, some silly sitcom, and Tony came home and said, in a perfectly normal upbeat tone of voice, 'What are you laughing at?' and I said, 'Oh nothing,' and flipped the TV off. I was all happy to see him and went right over to hug him. I put my arms around him—and shock! He didn't put his arms around me.

"I was so surprised. I backed away from the embrace and said, 'What's wrong?' and he just looked at me, impassive. 'If you don't know,' he said, 'I'm certainly not going to tell you.' 'Huh?' I said. 'What are you talking about?' He said nothing, just gave me an icy look, and then asked in a voice that matched his look, 'What are we doing for dinner?'

"I was astounded, Dr. Noelle. What had happened to my friendly, exuberant loving partner? Who was this frigid, mean individual? I tried to get him to talk, to say what was wrong, but he wouldn't budge. He was distant, polite, and cold for the next two days. The more he got distant, the more panicked I got. I couldn't sleep, I couldn't eat, I was barely functioning. I would beg and plead and cry to try to get him to tell me what was wrong, but nothing worked. He would just stare at me, wait until I was finished or exhausted, and then ask something totally mundane, like 'What time are you going to the market?'

"Finally, on the third day, as we were sitting eating dinner (he was eating, I was dying), he said, after carefully wiping his mouth with his napkin, 'Don't ever do that to me again.' 'Do what?' I asked very gently, scared of saying the wrong thing and his going silent again. 'Don't you ever dismiss me like that again,' he said. 'Dismiss you?' I asked, very gently once again. 'Yes, dismiss me,'

Tony repeated, 'Like say "Oh nothing" when I ask you what you're laughing about or thinking about or anything else like that. I don't like that. I don't like it one bit.' 'OK,' I said. I wasn't about to dare to say anything that might close off the small opening he'd just made back into our normal life. 'Good,' he said, getting up from the table. 'Let's do the dishes.'

"Tony was still cold to me that night, but over the next few days, he softened up and we were back to our 'normal' lifestyle together. Only after that, I never felt quite as comfortable and secure around him. Because it did happen again, you know. I would say something that I would never have considered dismissive or rejecting, but that's how he would take it, and I'd be in for a week of Arctic frost. I hated it. His distancing was more hurtful to me than anything he could have said or done."

"Did you two talk the situation over together?" I asked. Peter shook his head, "I tried to talk to him once about how much it hurt me when he'd go cold like that. I asked if maybe we could talk about whatever he thought I'd said that was dismissive before he got that way, and maybe we could clear the matter up before it got so hurtful. I really poured my heart out and let him see the pain. He was very quiet the whole time I talked, then his eyes took on that awful iciness, and he just said 'It's your pain, not mine. You bring it on yourself. You know exactly what to do to avoid it,' and walked out of the room.

"I felt knifed. I was stunned. There was clearly nothing he intended to change about his behavior, regardless of how it impacted me. If anything, he was completely righteous about his behavior. As far as he was concerned, it was only natural for him to behave that way, given what I had done." Peter stopped, then looked directly at me and said, tears rising in his voice, "I didn't ask for him to discuss it with me after that. I never wanted to risk that kind of hurt again."

THE WICKED WITCH OF THE NORTH

Teri's step had a bounce in it when she came in for her session. "I got a raise," she announced, all excited. "Good for you," I said, smiling. I was happy for her. Getting a raise would help validate Teri's feelings of self-worth, which were still very damaged from her experience with Anne. "So, are you ready to tackle another side to the Anne saga?" I asked. "Hey," Teri said, half joking, "I'm strong, lay it on me." "OK," I said, "let's look at what it was like in the beginning of the relationship when Anne wasn't being your delightful best friend. "Oh," said Teri, "you mean when Anne turned into the Wicked Witch of the North?" "That sounds about right," I said. "Hmmm," Teri said, growing thoughtful. She sat quietly for a moment, then began to speak: "I guess you'd call Anne 'moody.' She could be perfectly fine and happy one day, and the next morning wake up in a horrible mood, sullen and mean and just plain ornery. Which would be fine if she'd just keep her moods to herself, but that wasn't Anne's style.

"When Anne was pissed, she was pissed at everybody. She'd come home grousing about the traffic, in a foul mood. If I tried to lighten things up, you know by saying 'Well, you know what it's like in the city,' or 'That bad, huh?' she'd turn on me, saying I wasn't listening to her, that it was horrible, and clearly I didn't care about her and her well-being, and she was fed up with always caring about others and nobody caring for her. I kid you not, that's where it would go to.

"I'd try to talk to her and show her how that wasn't so, that I did care, but it only seemed to make her angrier. She would yell at me and just get madder and madder until she'd go into her room and slam the door. She'd huff and stomp around and generally be pissy for a while, and then just as suddenly as the anger had come on her, it'd be gone. She'd laugh and say, 'Wanna grab a beer?' or some such excuse, and she'd be all light and fun again. It was all very confusing."

"Did you try to talk to Anne about it?" I asked Teri my by now standard question. Teri laughed, "If I tried to talk to Anne about how she'd behaved, she'd just toss it off and say 'Oh, that' and refuse to discuss it. It was like it didn't matter. She was being however she wanted to be whenever the mood struck her, and that was that."

Case Analysis

Life with a potentially violent person is like walking through a mine field. You never know when there's going to be an explosion. These individuals don't get angry, they get enraged. They aren't disappointed, they pout for days. Their mood swings are totally unpredictable. This volatile behavior, so characteristic of abusers, has several highly recognizable aspects, each of which can serve as a warning sign for you.

RECOGNIZING THE DR. JEKYLL– MR./MS. HYDE SYNDROME

Life is good. You've been seeing this new person— friend or lover—for a month or so, and he or she is just wonderful. The relationship is everything you'd ever hoped for, this is the man/woman/friend of your dreams. Then suddenly, in the blink of an eye, this person turns into a monster, and you don't have a clue as to why or how this came about. You are horrified: What happened to your new lover or friend? What happened to that attentive, caring individual? Where did this mean, nasty, punishing individual come from? It doesn't make sense. You rack your brains trying to figure out what went wrong, generally trying to figure out what you did wrong. The answer is you did nothing wrong; at least nothing that would elicit this reaction from most people. You have just encountered one of the primary distinguishing characteristics of abusive individuals, the "Dr. Jekyll–Mr. Hyde" syndrome.

As cliched as it may sound, "Dr. Jekyll–Mr. Hyde" is the best phrase to describe the quick and dramatic personality change common to abusers. There are four components to this syndrome. Abusive individuals will display any one or several of these components to varying degrees. Each of the components serves as a warning sign.

EMOTIONAL OVERDRIVE

We are all capable of going into a deep depression, getting extremely angry, or withdrawing from our loved ones. There is nothing unusual about these behaviors. We are all capable of going into these emotional states very rapidly. That too is nothing particularly unusual. Where abusers differ from others is not in the strength or quickness with which they react, but the disproportionate or exaggerated nature of their reaction.

For example, you have a noon lunch appointment. You get there at 11:55 a.m., and your friend isn't there. You wait. You're a little surprised as 12:05 rolls around, since your friend is usually very prompt. As the clock marks 12:10, you're a little irritated, you have a 1 p.m. appointment down the street and you don't like to rush your lunch. When your friend arrives at 12:15, out of breath, and apologizes for being late, you grumble a little, then drop your irritation and have lunch. Your emotional reaction, irritation, is proportionate to what happened, a minor readjustment of your lunch time. An abuser in the same situation, however, is likely to get completely irate, throw her napkin on the ground, tell the offending friend that she will not put up with being treated this way, and stomp out of the restaurant. This is an emotional reaction disproportionate to the event.

John's sulking for three days, refusing to talk to Mary for days on end other than to make snide or distancing comments, sitting in the dark playing depressing music, drinking to excess, and not making it to work on time all constitute an emotional reaction disproportionate to the actual event.

Alcohol Abuse and Domestic Violence

The connection between alcohol abuse and domestic violence is well documented. If you are involved with an individual who drinks as a response to frustration or upset, that is a clear warning sign. Be alert! "Individuals who use alcohol and drugs are more prone to violence than those who don't. Alcohol and other drug abuse precipitates violence in 50 percent or more of all domestic abuse."[1] Fifty percent is far too great a percent to ignore. Drinking to alleviate stress and cope with problems is part of a larger pattern of dysfunction. It interferes with abusers' ability to appropriately process and communicate emotional issues to their partners. Drinking facilitated John's emotional overreactivity to the situation since it interfered with his ability to reason and assess the situation with some degree of objectivity or sense of perspective.

"When he finally told me what had made him so upset, Dr. Noelle, I was very confused," Mary said "He was in such an emotional state that I kept looking for something really major—like maybe he thought I was stepping out on him, or he'd lost his job, or he'd found out he had leukemia. When he said it was because of the 'call-waiting hang-up' episode, I was floored. How could something so unimportant be such a big deal?" Good question! "It's a big deal, Mary," I replied, "because it's not about the phone call or the hang up, per se. It's about betrayal." "Betrayal?" Mary exclaimed. "I don't get it. How could this possibly be about betrayal?"

Events Defined as Personal Rejections

I then explained to Mary how abusers do not see events through objective eyes; abusers define events in terms of how those events are or are not personally rejecting of them. *This is the potentially violent individual's main emotional focus* and is most easily expressed as follows: "Is this event or situation proof of my loved one's 100 percent total and complete attention and devotion to me 24 hours a day, or does it in some way demonstrate that my love's attention and devotion is less than 100 percent?" Anything less than 100 percent will be met with an extreme reaction from the abuser. Once you understand this is the way abusers view the world, a lot of their apparently incomprehensible behavior becomes easy to understand.

For example, the strength of Karen's outburst over the "kid in the store" incident was completely unwarranted by the actual event, when seen through objective eyes. However, it makes perfect sense, seen through the abuser's lens of betrayal. When Bob, attempting to defuse the situation, said that the kid's staring at Karen was "nothing" (pointing out the likely objective reality of the event), Karen interpreted his words as betrayal. He had failed to support Karen's irritation with the boy. To abusers, anything less than complete and unquestioning support of their every word and action is betrayal. The vehemence of Karen's reaction, screaming at Bob, yelling, storming out of the store, finally kicking the tires on his car, is understandable when seen as responses to betrayal. The problem is, abusers define as betrayal all sorts of situations and events that other individuals would not consider as such, even for a moment.

Lack of Constant Attention Equals Rejection

For example, in Mary and John's situation, John interpreted Mary's request to eat dessert later so as to go to a show on time as meaning everything was more important to her than him. This reaction is absurd by normal standards of what constitutes rejection. However, given that the abuser needs to be the focal point of his or her loved one's attention at all times, it makes perfect sense for the abuser to feel rejected when that attention is taken off, even for the briefest moment.

"Wow," said Mary, "I never would have thought of it that way, but it makes sense. I remember this one time, I was at the company picnic, we have it once a year. It's really nice, everybody comes from all the stores in the area. Anyway, I was there with John, standing in line to get food at the picnic tables, waiting my turn. One of the other cashiers, a guy, came over to where I stood and said, 'Hi, how ya doin'?' as he was on his way to take his place in line. Without thinking anything of it, since I was standing right by the plates table, I handed him an empty plate. Well, John, who was standing right behind me, was *incensed* that I had handed my co-worker a plate before handing him one, and accused me of not loving him. I just stood there with my mouth hanging open. I was amazed. I couldn't understand why he got so angry and how he could say that. But with what you're saying, it makes sense." "Yes," I said, "John felt betrayed." "But it was such a small thing," Mary said, "and I didn't mean it the way John took it at all." "What you meant by handing the plate to your co-worker, and how anybody else would have defined the incident, is irrelevant, Mary," I said. "John defined the incident as betrayal, and that's what determined his emotional response."

Failure to Share All Equals Rejection

There are many behaviors abusers define as rejection or betrayal that ordinary people would not put in such terms. Abusers typically expect you to be willing to share your every thought and feeling with them upon request. Since abusers feel they "own" you, as discussed in Chapter 5, they do not grant you the privacy ordinarily accorded by partners in a relationship of those thoughts and feelings you prefer to keep to yourself. This is the source of Tony's rage when Peter responded "Oh, nothing" to Tony's "What are you laughing at?"

Abusers expect you to give them access to all your thoughts and feelings at any given moment. Anything less than that is defined as betrayal and lack of love. To be dismissed, as Tony interpreted Peter's failure to answer him, is a capital offense. "Seen in that light," said Peter, "I understand his reaction, Dr. Noelle. But I still think it's way out there, it's not normal." Peter's right; such a reaction is not a normal one in a healthy relationship.

Abusers not only expect you to be willing to share your every thought and feeling, they also expect those thoughts and feelings to be unequivocally supportive and validating of them. Anne, for example, defined as rejection Teri's failure to appropriately commiserate with

Anne's unhappiness over that day's heavy traffic, or whatever else Anne was unhappy about. If Teri didn't immediately side with Anne and agree that the world was treating Anne miserably, she would turn and blow up at Teri.

UNPREDICTABLE EMOTIONAL REACTIONS

One of the most disconcerting aspects about being in a relationship with abusive individuals is the unpredictability of what is going to make them upset. Certainly, abusers get upset for the same reasons as the rest of us—a loved one says something deliberately hurtful, something goes wrong on the job, a friend fails to repay a debt. Being upset over these situations is predictable. But abusers also get upset, as described earlier, for events and situations they define as rejection and betrayal that would not be defined as such by most people, and that's where the unpredictability comes in.

The Abuser's Definition of Betrayal

"How was I to know John was going to get upset over my handing a plate to someone?" Mary exclaimed. "I couldn't have figured out that one in a million years." Mary is right, she couldn't have. John's definition of betrayal was not a commonly shared perception. It is the very personal and subjective nature of how they define rejection and betrayal that makes abusers' emotional outbursts unpredictable.

"It made me crazy," Bob said. "I'd think I'd pretty much figured out all the things that upset Karen, and then I'd do something innocuous, like pick up her shoes from the hall and put them in the bedroom, and she'd be screaming at me that I was trying to show her up as being messy, like couldn't I stop being Mr. Clean for a minute?" Bob sighed. "So, fine, the next time I saw her shoes in the hall, I left them there. Then Karen yelled at me for not being considerate of how tired she was, and not even having the decency to help out by taking her shoes into the bedroom." Bob laughed, "It sounds ridiculous now when I say it to you, Dr. Noelle, but at the time it felt just awful." It is awful. You no longer feel safe enough to live your life normally, without risking upset from your partner. You start walking more and more on eggshells.

You Sacrifice Your Truth

"It got so I was watching everything I said," Peter told me, "I hated it. I found it hard to relax and just enjoy him even when Tony was in a happy place, because I was so scared I'd say something that would get him upset. It was exhausting." Walking on eggshells is not only exhausting, it is also detrimental to the normal development of a relationship. How can a relationship grow in the absence of honesty? When you're scared to say anything in case your partner gets upset, you sacrifice your truth to their upset. The relationship becomes more and more about the abuser: In order to stay in the relationship, you must accept and go along with the abuser's perceptions and definitions of the world, regardless of how differently you see things.

INABILITY TO LET GO

There is a truism in psychology: "Anything you focus on grows." If you spill water on your friend's outfit at lunch, and you then focus on what a fool you are, how clumsy you were, what a general mess you make of things, and so on, I guarantee by the end of the day you will have thoroughly damaged your self-esteem, feel lower than dirt, and will probably do half a dozen things to prove what a worm you are. If, however, you spill the same water, but simply apologize to your friend, clean up the mess, and then switch your focus to resuming the conversation you were having before the spill, your self-esteem will emerge unscathed, you'll feel fine, and you'll have a normal day. This is the power of switching focus or letting go of a painful event in order to go forward with a more joyous life.

Growing the Pain

Abusers have great difficulty letting go of perceived slights and hurts. Abusers ruminate emotional pain. They focus on that pain, think about it, in silence usually, and rehash it until what possibly began as a small hurt assumes massive proportions. John, for example, nursed his pain over the "call-waiting hang-up call" incident and grew it for days, growing increasingly depressed and withdrawn. Tony maintained his icy rage over Peter's "Oh, nothing" response by staying focused on the incident for days.

Refusal to Talk

As is typical of abusers, both John and Tony refused to talk about what was going on with them to their respective partners. When you won't talk about something with your partner, that something is free to grow within you. There is nothing to counter or oppose your definition of how you got hurt, nothing to help soothe your hurt or facilitate healing. This is one way of refusing to let go of the hurt.

Refusal to Listen

Karen's way of hanging on to her hurt was different. She was very willing to express how she felt to Bob. However, she was unwilling to listen to anything he had to say that might help her either understand what he had said or done or to heal her from her hurt. Furthermore, Karen would return to the hurt and bring it up repeatedly, either unwilling or unable to release the hurt or allow it to subside.

Abusers' inability to let go of pain is a significant, although certainly not the only, contributing factor to their subsequent violence. In this process of reviewing, rehashing, focusing on, and eventually obsessing over the perceived slight or hurt, abusers frequently blow it up to such magnitude that violence seems only appropriate.

EMOTIONAL JUSTIFICATION

Abusers do not take responsibility for the impact of their emotional reactions on others. Even if they apologize and appear remorseful after inflicting physical pain, as we will see in Chapter 15, abusive individuals still feel righteous about their anger, sulking, and other emotional reactions. If there is a bottom line to how abusers justify their emotional outbursts, it is this: The only feelings that matter, are theirs.

Mary, for example, tried over and over to talk with John about how hurtful his pouts and sulks were, how miserable and difficult they were for her, yet his only answer was "too bad." Peter repeatedly told Tony how

hurtful his punishing silence was, but Tony was unconcerned. Bob tried to talk with Karen about the hurt and
confusion her behavior caused him, but she was uninter-
ested in her impact on him. Anne would just brush Teri
off, not caring about how her behavior affected Teri.

Regardless of how inappropriate, exaggerated, or
hurtful to their loved ones abusers' emotional reactions
are, abusers always feel justified in their reactions. If anything, abusers will maintain that they are being quite
civilized about their reactions, considering how betrayed
and hurt they feel. This position allows abusers to justify
highly inappropriate and hurtful behaviors regardless of
the consequences to others.

NOTE

1. Jerry Brinegar, *Breaking Free from Domestic Violence*, Comp-
    care Publishers, Minneapolis, Minnesota, 1992.

EIGHT

How to Work with Your Partner's Emotional Extremes

EXAGGERATED EMOTIONAL RESPONSES

Abusers have exaggerated emotional reactions to any situation in which they feel rejected, slighted, or dismissed. These reactions include quick and sudden mood swings, week-long sulks or pouts, and intense anger or rage. They run hot and cold with "hot" expressed as yelling, screaming, kicking, and throwing and "cold" as withdrawal, extreme distancing, the cold shoulder, and bottomed-out depression.

If your lover or friend displays sudden mood shifts or reactions that are clearly out of proportion to the event, imagined or otherwise, be on the alert. "But Dr. Noelle," you say, "How am I to know what is out of proportion? I can't know how much he is hurting. Maybe I said something horrible that really got to him." Maybe you did. It's your job to figure that out. Only then can you assess whether or not your lover or friend's reaction is disproportionate.

The Value of Common Sense

Use your common sense. If your lover grouses for an hour or so because you're going off without her on a fun vacation with some friends over the weekend, that's not unreasonable. If, however, your lover goes into a deep depression over your time off, accusing you of being selfish, cold-hearted, and never thinking of him, and won't talk to you for a week, his reaction is disproportionate to the event. Such a strong reaction would be more proportionate to being dumped!

Don't doubt your own good judgment of what is "out of proportion." If you think your lover's reaction is exaggerated, it probably is. Trust that. "Yes," you say, "but what if I'm wrong?" Well, that's what friends are for, among other things. Talk with your friends and family; run the situation by them. Take a poll: How would your friends and family assess the situation? If asked for honest feedback, they will generally give it. Not being involved as you are, they may have a more accurate sense of the situation.

Responding to Emotional Reactions

Don't automatically assume that just because your lover is reacting strongly, you are responsible. There are endless ways people can deal with hurt. Passive partners are unusually willing to take responsibility for other people's emotions; guard against that. Certainly, you may have contributed, intentionally or unintentionally, to your partner's pain, but how he reacts to that pain is his choice.

"What do you mean, choice?" you exclaim. "How can the way you react to something be a choice? Isn't reaction an automatic thing?" *Reaction* may be an automatic thing, yes, but how people *respond* to their reactions, what they then do with that reaction, is a matter of choice. You may have a reaction to someone saying something nasty to you, an automatic feeling of being hurt, but nowhere is it written that you are then biologically driven to sulk for a week. Some people sulk, some people laugh it off, some people talk about it with their partners. The possibilities are endless. Your lover's over-the-top reaction is a chosen one, and it will help you assess the situation more accurately if you keep that in mind.

Emotional Reactivity Is Not a Measure of Love

Don't equate great love and passion with great emotional reactivity. Overly intense emotional reactions are generally indicative of immaturity or psychological dysfunction, not true love. Don't buy into your lover's declaration: "If I didn't love you this much, I wouldn't react this way." Part of genuine love is a willingness to stay connected and communicate through the difficult times, through the hurts and upsets we inevitably cause each other. Severe emotional reactions separate people and make communication difficult, if not impossible.

Observe, Observe, Observe

Distance yourself emotionally as best you can from your lover's reaction and try to objectively observe what she is doing. Ask yourself, "Is this how I want a significant other in my life to respond to things? Can I live in this type of emotional climate? Is this type of reaction OK by me?"

Don't diminish the validity of your discomfort, confusion, or pain over this type of emotional reaction. Your feelings are trying to tell you something! If your lover is reacting this intensely to something relatively minor, how do you think she is likely to respond in the face of something major? Violence may be all that's left.

UNPREDICTABLE EMOTIONAL REACTIONS

Because abusers have highly personalized definitions of what constitutes rejection, you cannot predict what their reactions will be to any given situation or event.

Rejections and Slights

Notice what your friend defines as a rejection or slight. Is her definition a common way to define what happened? Ask yourself if you would define the situation the same way. "Gosh, I don't know," you say, "maybe I'm just thick-skinned, maybe my friend is just so sensitive that every little thing hurts her." If that's so, is this comfortable for you? Do you want to be involved with someone for whom so much of life is painful? "Isn't that cruel?" you ask. "Shouldn't I want to stand by my friend regardless of how sensitive she is?" Yes, of course, if all we were talking about was sensitivity, but we are discussing sensitivity expressed in a way that is very upsetting to you. Let me turn the question around: why would you want to spend your life walking on eggshells? What does that say about your desire to love yourself, respect yourself, give yourself freedom to be and grow as you choose? Freedom to be and grow is incompatible with walking on eggshells.

The Danger of Silence and Secrecy

Once again, talk to your friends and family. They can be much more objective than you in this situation. Rely on your friends to help you understand whether your friend's definition of a situation as a "slight" is a common one. "I can't talk to my friends about these things!" you exclaim. Then you are in deep trouble. Silence and secrecy are the two biggest reasons abuse flourishes. If you are unwilling to be open with those few people really close to you as a relationship develops, you deprive yourself of extremely valuable feedback. Passive partners tend to think everything that goes wrong in a relationship is their fault. If you're not willing to talk to someone about what is going on, chances are you'll think your friend's emotional overreactions are legitimate and that you are obviously a completely insensitive individual not to have realized how deeply you hurt her. You will have little realistic assessment of the situation. Don't allow yourself to be trapped in your own potentially erroneous thinking. Your friends and family love you and genuinely want the best for you. Be willing to talk things over with them and listen to what they have to say.

Crazy-Making

Another aspect of abusers' unpredictable reactions is their changeability. In other words, something that abusers had never objected to before suddenly becomes objectionable. "You made the bed wrong," he may say. "I've been making the bed this way for the past six months," you respond, confused. Your partner shoots you a look of intense hate and walks off. You know what that look means. You groan; here comes a week of cold withdrawal. This aspect of the abuser's unpredictable reactions is crazy-making. In a healthy relationship, partners get to know one another's preferences. You learn over time what the other person likes, and people tend to be consistent with their preferences. So if he likes the bed made a certain way in January, chances are he will like the bed made the same way in May. If one partner changes his mind and wants to try something different in the realm of bed-making, he will usually talk about it with the other. At the very least, he will simply respond to "Gee I thought you liked the bed made this way" with "Yeah, I did, I just felt like trying something different" and not blow up, sulk, or withdraw.

Abusive individuals, however, are not reacting to a preference, but to a buildup of internal pressures usually completely unrelated to the subject at hand. Therefore, abusers are very likely to react strongly to something they have up until now seemed perfectly content with because in truth, their reaction has little to do with the matter at hand. The eruption over the bed-making may be, for example, an outgrowth of the abuser's insecurity about his or her lovability or self-worth. The bed-making just serves as a trigger for an emotional explosion that was in the works, ready to come out at any time. Since you have no way of knowing when or what is going to set your partner off, you are always at risk of emotional reactivity.

What's the Pattern?

Observe your partner's patterns. Does he tend to go along with something for a period of time only to suddenly not like or want that thing anymore? More importantly, does your lover express not wanting or liking something in an emotionally overreactive way?

The relationship with an abusive individual inevitably ends up being one-sided. The active partner does all the "being sensitive" and emotional overreacting and the passive partner does all the "walking on eggshells" and "understanding." In a healthy relationship, there is room for both partners to be sensitive, for both partners to express themselves emotionally without damaging the other, and for both partners to be understanding of the other.

INABILITY TO LET GO

Abusers either hang on to a hurt, imagined or otherwise, for days, months, years, or they *apparently* drop it, only to come back to the same hurt again and again. Either way, they don't truly let go.

Hanging on to Hurt

If you find your friend has a tendency to hang on to a hurt, pay attention. Notice how long she hangs on to a hurt, or how often she comes back to it. Don't be fooled into believing that how long a person hangs on to a hurt or how often he comes back to it is indicative of how badly he was hurt. Not so. The amount of time an individual hangs on to a hurt or the frequency with which he returns to it only shows how unwilling he is to heal himself and the situation.

"Really, now, Dr. Noelle, that's ridiculous," you say. "Hurt is hurt, it takes time to heal, there's nothing you can do about that." Certainly it takes time to heal, yes, but more than that it takes *willingness* to heal. What is your friend doing in the service of that healing? Sitting and pouting, ruminating while listening to depressing music, or running the event over and over again in one's head isn't healing. It's amplifying the hurt. Does your friend seek to talk about her hurt, either with you or with other friends, a counselor, minister, shaman, anybody? Does your friend talk about how the hurt is helping her learn something new about herself or how it is helping her grow within? Is she seeking to understand why the hurt had such emotional impact? Only if your friend does this type of processing will she be able to heal the hurt, release it, forgive, and move on. And yes, all this takes time. But it is a very different use of time than reviewing the same material over and over again.

Coming Back to the Hurt

If your lover seems to drop the hurt right away, only to come back to it repeatedly, talk about it. Your lover may not be aware how much he brings up the issue, and therefore may not be aware of the healing that needs to be done. Notice how he reacts to your suggestion that there may be some healing to be done. In a healthy relationship, your partner may not be overjoyed by the idea, but will be willing to think about it. Abusive individuals will deny responsibility for self-healing and will say their failure to heal is because they are so hurt.

Taking Responsibility for Healing

Willingness to take responsibility for healing and to actively process issues to heal them is essential to the health of a relationship. We all hurt each other when in close relationships; it's inevitable. You try not to, but hurt happens. It becomes important to be able to release and heal with some degree of ease. Ask yourself, "Do I want to live in an atmosphere of hanging on, of grudges, of unfinished business?" Such an atmosphere can only be detrimental to the growth of a loving relationship. If you never release any of the old hurts, the relationship becomes one of rehashing old business and little energy is available for the relationship to develop in a positive direction. The relationship stagnates in an ever-growing mass of negativity.

Passive partners, never wanting to rock the boat for fear of losing the loved partner, often dismiss the abuser's hanging on to old hurts, saying, "Oh that's just the way he is." Maybe it is, but that spells trouble for you. Don't lull yourself into a false sense of security, thinking the abuser will stop at the ruminating and hanging-on stage. Nursing old wounds is one of the primary ways abusers get the necessary fuel to propel themselves into violence.

EMOTIONAL JUSTIFICATION

Abusers always feel justified in their emotional reactivity. If anything, they feel they have not given full expression to the degree of their hurt.

People Who Justify

Be leery of persons who justify their every action and behaviors, especially when those actions and behaviors are hurtful to another. In a healthy relationship, each partner is concerned about the happiness and well-being of the other and seeks to minimize the infliction of pain.

"But Dr. Noelle," you ask, "isn't it normal to be upset when your partner has hurt you?" Of course it is. What isn't normal in the sense of "healthy" is to refuse to work with your partner on the issue at hand and to maintain an emotional response that your partner has clearly told you is damaging to him or her.

One-Sided Dealing with Upsets

For example, your lover is upset because you went off to the movies without leaving a note saying where you were or when you would be back. This breaks an agreement the two of you had about letting each other know your whereabouts. Your lover has reason to be upset. However, she then proceeds to shout at you, telling you what an inconsiderate person you are, storms into the bedroom, slams the door, and refuses to talk about it, or to you, until the next day. At that time, your lover still won't listen to what you have to say, tells you if you're upset, "It's your own damn fault," and things get mighty awkward around the house for the next few days until she comes out of it and things get back to normal. This kind of response is typical of an abusive individual.

Dealing with Upsets Together

In a healthy relationship, your lover may be just as upset with the broken agreement; however, she would be willing to listen to your side of things and would not cut off further communication by stomping, storming, and slamming doors. If she did stomp, storm, or slam, she would at some point be willing to listen to you tell her how hurtful that is to you and would try to work with you on alternative, less damaging ways to express her hurt. Your lover would not justify her emotional response as right and immutable.

Notice that what makes the difference between how an abusive individual handles this sort of situation and how a nonabusive individual handles the same situation is the willingness to talk things over with the partner. Everybody gets upset, everybody occasionally goes overboard with their emotions. Nonabusive individuals recognize their overreactivity for what it is, take responsibility for it, and are willing to talk about it and attempt to change those behaviors that are hurtful to their partners. They do not sit on their righteousness.

Righteousness

Don't buy into your partner's righteousness. It is not acceptable to inflict major emotional reactivity on those around you. It is not appropriate, it is not kind, and it certainly is not loving. There are many other ways of dealing with hurts, real or imagined. If your lover is unwilling to sit down and communicate with you, actively seeking other ways to deal with hurts, yours as well as hers, then you don't have a relationship. You have the one-on-one equivalent of a dictatorship where your lover makes the rules and you follow them. Your lover does whatever he or she wants and you must accept that. Such a relationship disintegrates all too frequently into domestic violence.

Blame

NINE

Whatever It Is, It's All Your Fault

ASSIGNING THE BLAME

Not My Problem

"I'm mad," Mary said, plunking herself down on the couch, obviously distressed. "What about?" I asked. "Well, the more I think about what we talked about last time, about John's unwillingness to discuss how much his sulking hurt me, the madder I get!" "It is infuriating," I empathized, "to have your feelings ignored like that." Mary continued, "The funny part is, it makes me feel better to get angry." "You're standing up for yourself, Mary," I responded, "by honoring your feelings, getting angry about John's failure to recognize his impact on you. That's healthy! That's empowering. Of course it feels good." Mary looked at me, confused. "But I thought being angry was hurtful in relationships." "No, Mary," I replied, "what hurts people in relationships isn't feeling or acknowledging their anger, it's what people choose to do with that anger, how they choose to express it—or fail to express it." "Hmm," Mary said, "I gotta think about that one. Anyway, the thing I wanted to talk to you about today was that hurting my feelings wasn't the only thing John wouldn't take responsibility for. The more I thought about it, the more I realized John hardly ever took any responsibility for things that didn't work out for him, even little things, silly things."

Mary stopped, took a sip of water, calmed herself down a bit, and then went on with her story. "At first I just thought John was cursed with the darndest luck. If he didn't get a promotion at work, it's because some other person was willing to kiss up to the boss, and he wasn't. If he didn't have enough cash on him to pay for his share of dinner, it's because the ATM was out of order. If John couldn't find his keys, it was because the cat played with them. It was always someone or something else's fault if things didn't go John's way.

"For the first few months, I commiserated with John; all these things really seemed as he presented them, out of his control. But then I started thinking about it: Maybe he didn't get the promotion because John felt that putting in overtime was beneath him, or because he thought the boss was stupid and didn't mind telling everyone else at work that, or because John always sought to see how little he could get away with doing and still be doing his job. I made the mistake of trying to point some of these things out to him, thinking I was being helpful, supportive of his career, boy, then it really hit the fan.

"Now John told me that if he was unwilling to do overtime, it was to spend more time with me—so it was my fault that he lost his chance at the promotion. He told the other employees that the boss was stupid because I was always encouraging him to speak his truth, be self-confident, say what was truly on his mind. He'd only done what I said, so if it cost him a promotion, whose fault was it? And in terms of seeing how little he could do and still be doing his job, didn't I stress how important it was to have good time management, and was it his fault if he was saving all his energy for me? What a selfish, inconsiderate bitch I was, he exclaimed, when he was only doing what I wanted, even when it cost him a promotion.

"By the time he was done, I was so confused, all I could do was start apologizing again." Mary shook her head, "I feel so stupid, Dr. Noelle, you'd think I could have figured out what was going on." "Mary," I replied, "it's not about stupid. You didn't know what John's behavior meant. You didn't have the knowledge you needed to figure out what was going on. That's not stupid, that's lack of information." "I know," Mary said, "I just wish I'd had that information then! Anyway," she continued, "I wanted to tell you about something else John did that hurt me very much. But you have to promise not to laugh." "OK," I said, somewhat surprised, "I promise not to laugh." "Because some of this is going to sound funny," Mary said, "but believe me, it wasn't funny at the time.

"When John would drink wine, he'd snore, really badly. And if he was in a funk about anything, he'd drink a couple of bottles, all on his own. Well, it got so I couldn't sleep. I'd tried all the old wives' remedies, like nudging him, rolling him on his side, and all that worked to a certain extent, but there were more and more times when there was nothing for it but for me to go and sleep on the couch in the living room. And I wouldn't sleep well, I'd be exhausted.

"I thought we could talk about it, but no way. John looked at me like I was crazy and said, 'I don't snore.' I said, 'You do too! I'm the one awake to hear it.' 'Then you're just too light a sleeper,' he answered. I was bound and determined to show him what I was talking about. I made a tape recording of his snoring the next time he did it. I swear it sounded like a chainsaw bringing a whole forest of trees down. But John refused to listen to the tape. John refused to acknowledge he had any part in this at all. And he adamantly insisted that my exhaustion was my fault, and I should go fix it."

Mary sighed, "John's response to anything I mentioned that was hurtful or distressing to me in the relationship was that it was my fault and I should go fix myself, Dr. Noelle. He was so convincing that for a long time, I thought he was right. I must have spent a fortune in time, effort, and money trying desperately to 'fix myself.' And here I am again, one more time, with you now, trying to 'fix myself,'" Mary said, as she started to cry. "No, Mary," I said gently, "you're not here to 'fix yourself.' There's nothing about you to 'fix.' You're here to heal, Mary, to heal—and to learn some information and some skills so this never happens again."

A Man In Pain

Bob started this particular session by talking about how badly he felt about his ability to do and be in the world. "My confidence is pretty much all shot, Dr. Noelle," said Bob, "I can't seem to get back to the way I felt about myself before I met Karen. Somewhere in that relationship, I just lost it." "How do you think that's connected to your relationship with Karen?" I asked. "In every way, Doc," Bob said, "in every way." "Can you explain that to me?" I asked, pushing a little. "Yeah, I think so," Bob said. "I'll give it a try, anyway."

He stopped a moment, collecting his thoughts, and then said: "Before living with Karen, I felt like a pretty OK guy. I knew I wasn't perfect, but I thought I was a decent sort. I was fairly self-confident; I knew I wasn't Superman, but I thought I was competent in the world, and I knew how to deal responsibly with people and relationships. Karen changed all that. By the time she was through with me I felt personally inept, relationship-impaired, and probably destined for a lonely life given how foolishly I ruined everything in her and my relationship. It was amazing how many of the bad things that happened to Karen were somehow my fault. I rarely could see the connection, but she always made sure I did by the time she was finished.

"When her car broke down because she'd never had the oil checked and had been running without oil for I don't know how long, it was my fault. Although she had never asked me to, we'd never discussed it, and I had never given it any thought on my own, Karen informed me that it's a man's job to take care of his wife's car and how dare I let her car run without oil and unsafely. Clearly I didn't give a damn about her by letting such a thing happen.

"When her dogs tore up the backyard and made a mess of the flower beds I'd just planted, dug their way under our fence, and ruined the neighbors' newly laid concrete patio, which we now had to pay for, it was my fault because I wouldn't let them stay in the house when we were out. I was a cold and awful man who cared nothing for the comfort of animals. The fact that I wouldn't let them stay in the house because Karen had failed to see to it that her dogs were properly trained, and they would poop and pee everywhere, was completely ignored.

"When Karen was fired from her job for being over an hour late to work a minimum of three days a week for over two months, it was my fault. If I didn't want to make love so much, she wouldn't be so exhausted that she overslept and would be late to work. The fact that Karen wanted to make love as much as I did, and that she'd usually stay up another couple of hours watching late night television afterwards while I slept contentedly away (with earplugs so I couldn't hear the TV), and she would dawdle happily over her morning bath, regardless of whether she was running late, never entered into her consideration. I was a chauvinist pig, messing up her life, inconsiderate male that I was.

"She was so good at it, I'd get all confused. I never thought I was that inconsiderate and unthinking, but here was the passionate, adoring woman in my life saying so. She was so convincing, I figured there must be some truth here. And I'd apologize and try to do better, but it never seemed to work, and I was still always to blame."

"After one of Karen's hysterical outbursts or blaming episodes, I would get real depressed. I could hardly eat or sleep, and I felt just awful." Bob stopped for a moment, then said, "She told me that it was my problem, not hers. Seemed pretty much everything was my problem ... Boy, I sound like a whiner, don't I Doc," Bob said, shaking his head. "No," said I, "you sound like a man in pain." "Yeah," said Bob, "a lot of pain."

Always the Bad Guy

Peter looked at me for a moment, considering my question. "Did Tony have a problem accepting responsibility?" he said, repeating my question. "Yeah, you could put it that way. Tony had a way of implying that things that went wrong were my fault. He'd rarely say it directly, but it was as if he held me personally responsible whenever something didn't go exactly the way he wanted it in his life. I remember when he didn't have enough money to put a payment down on an outfit he was trying to buy. He said, in that awful sarcastic way of his, 'Hope you really enjoy the new air conditioner.' It took me a moment, but then I figured out what he meant was that somehow it was my fault for wanting a new air conditioner that he couldn't afford the payment for the outfit he wanted. When I reminded him that he was the one who insisted we get a top-of-the-line, very expensive air conditioner rather than an ordinary one, he came back with 'Oh, I see, we're supposed to buy crappy appliances for the house. No, that's fine, that's good, I'll remember that.' Suddenly the whole thing was turned around and I was the bad guy not only for the cost of the air conditioner, but also for not appreciating his eye for quality. He was miserable all because of me, and man did I pay for it . . . a week's worth of Tony being distant, cold, and aloof.

"Nowhere, by the way, in all of this, did he say directly it was my fault that he couldn't afford the payment for the outfit. If I had confronted him and said 'Do you mean it's my fault you don't have enough money?' he would have said, 'What are you talking about? You're really wacked, you know.' It was crazy-making. I got to where I just accepted the blame, implied or otherwise, and tried to get past the bad times as best I could."

The Little Things

Teri noticed Anne's tendency to blame in a different arena: "It wasn't so much the big things," Teri said. "Anne didn't try to blame me for her job, or things like that. But she would blame me for all sorts of little things, and it ended up driving me nuts. If the pizza delivery was late, it was my fault because I called the wrong pizza place, even if I had called her favorite. If she ran out of gas and forgot to tank up, it was because she'd been thinking about what I'd like for my birthday and gotten distracted. I mean it was ridiculous! If she ate my food in the fridge (we split the shelves, hers–mine), it was because I had made the decision on which shelf was whose and she just kept getting confused. And it went on and on. Eventually I stopped trying to defend myself, and just started going with the flow. All I could think was for her very terrific upsides, Anne sure had some strange downsides."

Case Analysis

Abusers consistently blame others for whatever goes wrong in their world. They also blame others for their feelings and their behavior. Even if at some later point abusers express remorse (see Chapter 15), they do not take responsibility for the behavior. Regardless of the circumstances, it is always somebody else's fault if abusers feel unhappy, angry, or upset.

YOUR PARTNER'S ROTTEN BEHAVIOR IS ALL YOUR FAULT

You are very confused. Up until a short while ago, you were walking on air, enjoying a quality and quantity of attention and affection you had only dreamed of before. Then your partner turns into some sort of monster, a Mr. Hyde character described in the previous chapter. You are confronted with a mean, vicious person you scarcely recognize. You don't want your dream to come crashing down. You don't want to believe that this person, who has been so loving, caring, and attentive until now, could possibly also be the icy/hysterical/mean individual in front of you. Your mind pushes that possibility away and tries to make sense of the situation. So when your partner tells you his upset is your fault, that you provoked such awful behavior, you are only too willing to accept this response. Most people would rather believe that their partner is a fundamentally good person whom they provoked into uncharacteristic mean behavior than admit that their partner is, in fact, a monster hiding behind a facade of apparently loving behavior. At least if it's their fault, most people feel that they can maybe do something to fix it, and then perhaps they can have their blissful relationship back. If the partner really is a monster, however, the loving relationship is over, and the person's dream is shattered. Longing to return to their original happiness, people often prefer to accept the blame.

What Accepting the Blame Does for You

Mary explained what it felt like to her: "By the time John was willing to talk to me again after three days of his being in this horribly depressed place, I was so grateful that I would have done anything. Even though there was a little voice in me saying, 'Wait a minute, this doesn't make any sense, how could I have ruined his day over something as small as an accidental hang-up, and how come he didn't talk to me about it right away?' I wasn't interested in listening to that voice, because if I did, it meant maybe there was something seriously wrong here, and I didn't want to look at that, I just didn't, Dr. Noelle."

Mary accepted the blame and apologized for John's emotional reaction as if she had caused it, thus setting up a dangerous dynamic. When you take responsibility for abusers' rotten behavior, you give them permission to do whatever they want, because from here on in, whatever they do, no matter how hurtful, is going to be defined as your fault. Consider that at this stage of the relationship, we're only talking about abusers pinning blame for their *emotional* reactions and acting out on the other. Imagine how much more horrible it is when an abuser says, "When I hit you, it's your fault. When I kick you, it's your fault. If you didn't incite me so, if you didn't treat me so poorly, if you were nice to me, I wouldn't do that. It's all your fault," never acknowledging that it is his hands doing the hitting, his feet doing the kicking. People have died hearing those words, thinking it must be their fault.

Keeping the Peace

"I can certainly see how Karen might interpret some of the things I said and did as slights against her," Bob said. "OK, it happens. But what I never was really convinced was my fault was the *enormity* of her upsets, of her emotional reactions." "Then why did you accept responsibility for the entirety of Karen's reactions?" I asked him. "I'm embarrassed to say this, Doc," Bob replied, "but I wanted to keep the peace and I loved her. I wanted my Karen back, the one I knew and loved, and I didn't care how I got her back. If I had to say it was all my fault, fine, OK, so it's all my fault." "You didn't see what you were setting up for down the road," I said. "No," Bob said, shaking his head, "I didn't see that at all."

And why should you? People don't expect a relationship that starts out so well to end up so horribly. People don't stop to think that if they say "OK, so it's my fault" to one thing in order to keep the peace and get the relationship back on track, they are setting a precedent for all future incidents. Within the context of a healthy relationship, that's not so! In the context of an abusive relationship, however, it often is.

Return to Mr./Ms. Wonderful

In some instances, once the passive partner has taken responsibility for the rotten behavior of abusers, the abusers feel absolved, and can return to their "Mr./Ms.

Wonderful" self. Such was Bob's experience with Karen. Almost as soon as he had taken her into his arms after the store incident and told her "It's all right, I love you," she cried and began to kiss him passionately. Once Peter had agreed to Tony's interpretation of the 'Oh nothing' incident described in Chapter 7, Tony began to thaw and soon their relationship was back to "normal." Both Mary and Teri experienced similar such returns to "normal" once they'd either agreed with or taken responsibility for their partner's behavior.

However, as this process continues through the relationship, the abuser finds it easier and easier to justify the abuse, and a dangerous downward cycle begins. The passive partner continues to accept the blame for the abuser's rotten behavior, which means that regardless of how rotten that behavior is, the abuser is repeatedly absolved. It's almost as if the more horrible the behavior, the holier the abuser gets and the more sullied the passive partner becomes. What starts in the beginning as a simple tactic to keep the peace becomes a hurtful, self-perpetuating mechanism of blame.

EVERYTHING THAT GOES WRONG IN YOUR PARTNER'S LIFE IS SOMEBODY ELSE'S FAULT (USUALLY YOURS)

Abusers suffer from very low self-esteem and a damaged sense of self-worth, which produce painful feelings and fears of both not being OK (a good enough human being) and not doing OK (good enough) in the world. They defend against the pain and fear by denying it, by declaring to themselves and everyone around them that they are perfect, that they do everything right. As long as life is going well and the abusers are getting what they want, their denial works.

However, life being what it is, not everything goes right all the time. Everybody makes mistakes, isn't prepared, does something stupid, and generally messes up. For most of us, this is not catastrophic. You know you goofed; you may feel less competent and confident for a while, but you try to figure out what you did wrong, what your contribution was to the mess. You learn from it, try to fix things, and move on. If your self-esteem and self-worth are based on denial of all imperfection, however, as is true for an abusive individual, you're in trouble. Any mistake, error, or incompetence becomes a critical threat to the abuser's already very damaged sense of self.

Projection

Abusers, faced with such threat, *project*. What this means is that in the absence of being able to accept their imperfections and mistakes and work toward bettering things, abusers project anything that goes wrong in their lives onto someone or something else. They do it in such a way that they come up innocent of all mistakes or wrongdoing. This is what led Mary, for example, to conclude that John had "the darndest luck." John's excuses for whatever went wrong always made him look good: He didn't get a promotion because he wouldn't "kissyup." How very noble of him. He didn't have enough cash because the ATM was out of order—who could fault him for that? John's keys must have been swiped by the cat, again, something quite out of John's control.

"I was so willing to believe him," Mary said. "It just sounded so plausible. I mean, those kinds of things do happen." And indeed they do—but not all the time to the same person. This is a key indicator you are dealing with an abuser: an individual's refusal to accept that although sometimes some of the things that go awry in our world can be attributed to others, most of the time we have something to do with it. A second key indicator is how abusers react when you suggest they might have something to do with the mishaps in their lives. Abusers do not tolerate being held responsible for the ill that befalls them. They distort a situation so that any responsibility they do accept puts them in a good light. Abusers will then shift responsibility for any part of the situation that might cast them in less than favorable light onto someone or something else. That someone else is, most often, you.

"I Did It All for You"

Mary first encountered this characteristic when she tried to talk with John about his failure to get a promotion. John took every one of Mary's observations (John's refusal to work overtime, saying his boss was stupid, doing as little work as possible) and turned them against her. They all became things he did to please Mary. John now looked not only pure, but martyred. How could Mary possibly fault him for doing something for her, which to boot had cost him a promotion? On the contrary, his failure was her fault.

"Why would he do that, Dr. Noelle?" Mary asked, frustrated. "Why blame me, of all people? I'm supposed to be the one he loved." "That's the very reason he blamed you," I began. "That doesn't make any sense to me," Mary interrupted, exasperated. "Think about it, Mary," I continued. "Who is pointing out his failure to him? Who is seeing him and therefore making him look at himself as less than perfect? He has to get himself off the hook somehow! Of course he's going to blame you, not because you had anything to do with the situation, but because you are making him look bad." "And all I was trying to do was help," Mary said sadly. "You were doing the best you knew how, Mary. With another type of individual, what you had to offer would have been received very differently," I said. "It just wasn't going to happen with someone like John."

Never Getting It Right

For Bob, bearing the brunt of Karen's blame became part of being in the relationship. "I just got used to it," Bob said. "If something went wrong, I could pretty much count on being blamed for it. It didn't really matter if it was the dogs, the traffic, Karen's day at work—it somehow all got to be my fault. After a while, I stopped trying to figure it out and just accepted it. She was so fantastic to be around when things were good, I thought 'I'll get better at this, I'll do things the right way and she won't go off on me.' I guess I fooled myself into thinking 'someday I'll get it right.'" You can't get it "right," though, because it isn't about you. It's about the abuser's inability to accept responsibility.

No-Risk Blame

Tony was less direct in the way he shifted responsibility onto Peter, not usually blaming him outright, but blaming him nonetheless. "What I don't understand, though, is why would Tony want to blame me? Why not pick on some neutral third party?" Peter asked, half jokingly. "It's safe to pick on you," I replied. "What do you mean?" Peter asked. "You're not likely to go anywhere, are you?" I said."You have a major investment in the relationship—your heart. You are more likely to accept blame than you are to leave, at least at this stage of the relationship. So it's safe to pick on you. Tony could absolve himself, slide you lower off the pedestal, feel holier-than-thou all without risking the relationship." "It worked for him," said Peter, understanding, "and you're right, I wasn't going anywhere."

Far-Fetched Blame

Abusive individuals almost invariably shift blame. If it's impossible to blame a significant other for a given situation, abusers will blame anyone and anything else, whatever it takes to take responsibility for failure off themselves. "I remember this one time," Teri said, "we were watching TV, flipping channels, and there was a program where they were interviewing some author. Apparently he'd written a really hot best-seller about life at his high school. Anne sat bolt upright and said, 'I know him. We were in school together.' She listened very intently to the rest of the interview and then turned the television off and slammed the remote down. Boy, was she mad! She said over and over that it wasn't right that the guy should have written the best-seller. She said she should have been the one to write it, that she could have written the book much better. She was convinced her classmate had somehow stolen her success from her. I couldn't believe my ears. Anne hadn't had any contact with this guy in 15 years, had never wanted to write a book that I knew of, and had certainly never talked about her high school days as being anything special. None of that seemed to matter. Somehow it was Anne's classmate's fault that Anne wasn't a best-selling author. She went on about it for days."

Abusers are remarkable in the way they stretch logic to turn responsibility for what happens to them away from themselves and onto others. Teri's description of Anne's blaming her classmate is not uncommon. We are all too quick to dismiss such far-fetched blaming as fantasies, too "out there" to mean much of anything. You don't stop to ponder what this kind of thinking implies about how that individual will behave in the course of a relationship.

YOUR DISTRESS AND YOUR PAIN OVER HOW YOUR PARTNER TREATS YOU ARE YOUR FAULT

In a healthy relationship, if your partner does something you experience as hurtful, you can go to your partner and talk about it. And granted, your partner may not be overjoyed to hear about the hurt she has caused you, but she will usually be willing to listen to you and be open to discussing ways of behaving differently in the future. This won't work with abusers. As far as abusers are concerned, anything bad that happens is not their fault, so clearly, if you're in pain, it can't be their fault. Abusers may say, "Gee, I'm sorry you feel that way" if you say you're unhappy or feeling neglected or are angry with them, but they won't consider that it has anything to do with them. No matter how logically you explain it, abusers will steadfastly maintain it's not their fault, and therefore refuse to participate in a solution.

In and of itself, this might be tolerable (although not healthy and not recommended in any relationship), but abusive individuals go one step further. Any hurt or distress you feel because of something the abuser did is— you guessed it—your fault. Mary's unhappiness over John's "sulks," as she called them, were Mary's fault in John's eyes. He was not concerned by the distress he caused her. John told Mary quite clearly that she was responsible for her own bad feelings. So too, when Mary approached John with the fact of his snoring, John was unconcerned with Mary's pain. John denied even the existence of his snoring and told Mary her exhaustion was her fault.

Only the Abuser's Feelings Matter

At this stage in the relationship, you start to feel like the only feelings that matter are your partner's. No matter what's going on, abusers find ways to make the issue about *their* feelings, not yours. Tony, for example, was very skilled at turning Peter's upsets into a reason for Tony to feel miserable. He forced Peter to deal with his feelings once again rather than seeking to deal with Peter's feelings. "We'd have plans," Peter said, "to meet somewhere after work. Tony wouldn't call to say he was going to be late. I'd be waiting, sometimes an hour, often an hour and a half. I'd be upset that he hadn't called, but when I'd tell him so, he'd blame me for ruining his evening by my being upset. He'd turn it around so, once again, it was all about him. We never dealt with my hurt feelings; it was always about Tony. Everything was always about Tony."

Indifference to Your Pain

Such callous lack of concern for the other's feelings is in direct contradiction with the abuser's stated love for his or her partner. It is a clear warning sign of an abusive relationship. Time and time again, abusers' indifference to the pain they cause is evident early on in the relationship. As described in Chapter 7, Karen was indifferent to Bob's pain over her emotional outbursts, Tony's only response to Peter's hurt over Tony's "iciness" was to tell him to quit bringing it on himself. Anne shrugged off Teri's complaints about her moodiness. Later in the relationship, this indifference becomes life-threatening: When abusers speak meanly to you, hit you, take your money, or rape your body, in their eyes it is still your fault.

TEN

How to Refuse Blame
that Doesn't Belong to You

YOUR PARTNER'S ROTTEN BEHAVIOR
IS ALL YOUR FAULT

Oddly enough, although abusers are the ones doing the abusing, they most often actually feel like victims. Abusers don't accept responsibility for their negative feelings or behaviors. Their basic stance in life is "They've done it to me," pointing the finger at the other person—generally you.

Take Responsibility Appropriately

When confronted with your lover's blame, stay grounded. Be honest with yourself. Most of us know when we have deliberately harmed another or can recognize if we have done harm without meaning to. Take responsibility when it is appropriate, but don't take it when it isn't.

"How can I know for sure that something is or isn't my fault?" you ask. "Things aren't always so clear-cut." True, some situations are confusing. In that case, think. Most of us don't think things through nearly as much as we could. "But I'm not that smart," you say. You're smarter than you realize. Deciding how much you are responsible in a given situation doesn't take years of schooling. All it takes is a willingness to sit down and figure it out. For example, your lover comes home, grumpy and out of sorts, generally in a rotten mood. He blames you, saying that he wouldn't have had a lousy day if the two of you hadn't argued that morning. "So it is my fault," you say. "I know I was the one to start the argument that morning." Maybe so, but think. Even if you started the argument in the morning, whose choice was it to let that argument affect his whole day? Did you refuse to discuss the issue with your lover and make it difficult for him to resolve it?

"No," you say, "actually, I thought the whole thing was resolved before we each left for work that morning. We kissed goodbye like we always do and everything seemed fine." "I see," I say. I continue to review what happened. Having announced that his rotten mood is all your fault, your lover proceeds to go systematically through a couple of six packs, get wasted, fall asleep on the couch, and blame you for his hangover the next day. "Well, it is sort of my fault," you say. "I mean, if he wasn't so upset, he wouldn't have been drinking." Really? Is drinking the only alternative to being upset? What happened to talking things through? If your lover was still upset, even though you felt everything had been resolved, couldn't he have opened his mouth and said something? And whose responsibility is it how much your lover drinks? Does one beer have to lead to many beers? Whose responsibility is it how many drinks caused your lover his morning-after hangover? Yours? No.

Think Things Through

Be willing to think things through. Go through the situation step by step. "All right, I can see where I was at fault here," and "No, this doesn't belong to me." Then talk to your partner about what you find, *not* in order to defend your innocence and proclaim his guilt, but in an attempt to work out a better understanding of what happened so each of you functions with more honesty toward the other. "You mean that's possible?" you exclaim. Of course it's possible. In a healthy relationship, you can say to your lover, "Honey, I realize I started the argument this morning and I apologize for that. It was a poor way of discussing what I was experiencing. I should have waited until later and brought the subject up when we weren't both rushed. I'm sorry. However, I don't feel comfortable with your blaming me for your rotten mood or your drinking or your hangover." Your lover may not like hearing this, but in a healthy relationship he will be willing to talk about it and will accept responsibility for what is his.

If at this early stage of the relationship, your partner is consistently unwilling to accept his share of responsibility for his rotten behavior, you are in serious danger of being involved with an abusive individual. Even if that abuse never erupts into physical violence, you are at risk of considerable emotional and mental abuse.

If you are in doubt as to whether you are being unfairly blamed, ask your friends and family or seek out the advice of a counselor.

Blaming the Victim

Don't ever buy into the myth that you have made someone behave in a certain way. Unless you hold a gun to someone's head (or the emotional equivalent of a gun, e.g., a life-threatening situation such as rape), people are responsible for their own actions. No matter how much you may have been responsible for a person's anger or hurt, it is still his or her choice what to do with it. The person can leave the room, try to talk with you about it, call up a friend or sponsor, throw things at you, or hit you. If your lover starts blaming you for his or her rotten behavior, watch out. Abusers are notorious for blaming the victim for their battering.

EVERYTHING THAT GOES WRONG IN YOUR PARTNER'S LIFE IS SOMEBODY ELSE'S FAULT (USUALLY YOURS)

Abusers make every unhappy situation in their life somebody else's fault. Whether it's not having enough money, being late to work, having a miserable headache, or having a lousy sex life, it doesn't matter. Whatever it is, it's always somebody else's fault.

Learning versus Blaming

"But a lot of people just have bad luck," you say. "I mean, sometimes it seems to happen all at once: The car breaks down, your cat dies, your best friend moves out of town, you get 'downsized,' you can't find a new job." Yes, but you don't have to make those things someone's fault. Nor do you have to see everything that happens to you as outside your sphere of influence. You can take advantage of the opportunity every single one of those events affords you not as opportunities to blame, but as opportunities to learn and grow.

Luck, it has often been said, is the outgrowth of skill and preparation. Both skill and preparation are self-generated. Bad luck might be thought of as the outgrowth of little skill and less preparation. For example, nonabusive individuals might look at the car breaking down as a reminder to pay better attention to the car's upkeep in the future or to start saving toward a new vehicle. Abusive individuals might say the car broke down because those idiots at the service station don't know how to do anything right. Which position leads to better luck next time?

Powerlessness Leads to Abuse

There is a recurring theme here: Abusive individuals do not take responsibility for their actions when those actions have negative consequences. It is one of the easiest ways to spot an abusive individual. People who feel the need to blame others do so because they feel powerless. Their low self-esteem and poor self-worth makes it difficult for them to feel confident about their ability to live life successfully, regardless of how loudly they may proclaim their wonderfulness on the outside. Powerless people are much more likely to resort to abuse than people who feel powerful.

Do not confuse power over others with genuine power. Genuine power has to do with the ability to accomplish what you want to accomplish. Power over others has to do with forcing or manipulating others into accomplishing for you what you cannot or will not accomplish for yourself. Truly powerful people work with others in order to accomplish goals, not by forcing or manipulating them.

The Sympathy Game

Notice where your lover places responsibility for all of life's woes. Don't play the sympathy game. Listen up! Ask yourself if what she is saying makes sense to you. Are all those things she is complaining about really someone else's fault? Or does she have at least a share in the responsibility?

Where's the Blame?

Then ask yourself: How does your lover deal with your suggesting that she may have something to do with what happened? For example, say you point out that if the car broke down, awful as that is, maybe it's a reminder to get to the service station more often. Your lover comes back at you with "Oh, great, love the support I'm getting here. So now it's my fault the car broke down." You may be dealing with an abusive individual. If the conversation continues along the lines of your saying,"No, I'm not saying that, what I'm saying is, it might be a good opportunity to review how you have been taking care of your car and see if you want to do anything differently in the future." If your lover's answer to that one is, "Oh, I see. Well, you've got a point there, I'll think about it," then you are probably not dealing with an abusive individual. If, however, your lover now starts in on you, making you responsible in the end for the car's breaking down, you are involved with an abusive individual. If abusive partners can't pin the blame on anyone else, they will invariably pin it on you. Simply being aware of this behavior and noticing its presence in your relationship will warn you of future abuse.

Avoiding Having to Change

Abusive individuals also blame someone else for whatever they don't like in their lives as a way of absolving themselves from having to resolve the situation. If you are in a relationship with a partner who feels no motivation to change anything about his life or how he behaves because it is not his fault, who do you think is going to end up having to make all the changes? Passive partners find themselves doing all the work of the relationship, as well as adjusting to all those things the abusive individual won't do anything about. Passive partners then wonder why they eventually get resentful or depressed. If abusers put the blame on other people for everything that isn't wonderful in their lives, they will at some time or other put that blame on you.

YOUR DISTRESS AND YOUR PAIN OVER HOW YOUR PARTNER TREATS YOU ARE YOUR FAULT

This is probably the area of blame that initially hurts passive partners the most. Abusers will not only blame you for whatever negative feelings they believe you inflicted on them, but they will also blame you for whatever negative feelings they caused you. In other words, their bad feelings are your fault, and your bad feelings are your fault. Any bad feelings anywhere in the relationship, regardless of who is feeling them or why, are your fault.

The Impossibility of Discussion

Your lover has finally come out of a week's worth of icy withdrawal. You try to talk to him about the pain that withdrawal caused you. Abusive individuals will not be open to any discussion, or, if they are willing to discuss it, the conversation will be limited to "It's your fault." An abuser will tell you, "You should know better than to irritate me." If you were hurt by the resultant "ice," too bad. In a healthy relationship, you can talk with your partner about the pain the withdrawal caused you. Even if he isn't thrilled about it, he will make an effort to hear you out, empathize with your pain, and try to work together toward ways of reacting that work better for both of you.

Your Unmet Wants and Needs

Other negative feelings that come up in a relationship have to do with your unfulfilled needs and wants. Expressing these needs and working with them is important to the development of a mutually satisfying relationship. How your lover deals with your expression of your unmet needs is indicative of whether you are involved with an abusive individual.

If, for example, your boyfriend has been spending most of his evenings for the past month on the couch, watching television, falling asleep there, and stumbling into bed somewhere in the middle of the night, you might say to him, "I miss you, I'm lonely, come spend some time with me." He looks up at you, maybe says "I'm sorry," and then goes back to watching television. You try again: "I'm lonely, I want to be with you." "So watch TV," he says, engrossed. You try watching TV for a while. The show he is watching ends. You say, "Let's spend some time together, I miss you, I'm lonely for you." He explodes, "So what the !@#$ does that have to do with me?! So you're lonely, so what? Leave me alone already." Off you crawl, ashamed, embarrassed at having revealed your vulnerability, your longing, and cry yourself to sleep.

Your bad feelings and your loneliness are a shared responsibility, one that has to do with both you and your partner. It is a matter of concern to both of you and would be discussed as such between partners in a healthy relationship. An abusive individual, however, refuses to share responsibility for a partner's emotional well-being and therefore refuses to even discuss it. All too often, passive partners end up feeling horribly ashamed any time they allow themselves to disclose vulnerable feelings. If you find yourself in such a situation, ask yourself if you want to be in a relationship with a person who refuses all emotional responsibility for the relationship. Imagine how that will affect your life together.

"Seeing the Light"

Don't mislead yourself by thinking you can reason with your lover until he "sees the light" or that you can somehow over time, with much love and patience, show him how the emotional responsibility is shared in a healthy relationship, at which point you're sure he'll be willing to do his part. If your lover were open to such reasoning, he would by now have seen enough "light" to assume responsibility for at least *discussing* the negative impact of his behavior on you. Choosing to dedicate your life to such a mission is all too likely to end up in disaster.

WARNING SIGN #5

Verbal Abuse

ELEVEN

Words that Hurt

DUMB AND STUPID

"You've talked a lot about how John's blaming you for anything and everything was very hurtful to you," I said to Mary during a session some weeks later. "Were there other aspects of the relationship with John around that time that you found to be hurtful?" I asked. "Yes," Mary answered, almost immediately, "his words." "His words?" I asked, not understanding. "His words got mean," Mary said. "He started criticizing me a lot, about all sorts of things, saying really mean things. It was strange, Dr. Noelle, when we first met, there was nothing about me he didn't like. Now it seemed more and more there was nothing about me he did like." "Can you elaborate?" I asked. Mary shrugged her shoulders, "I mean, I know the honeymoon can't last forever. I know at some point you start to see how people really are and you don't like all of it, but John seemed to go from loving everything about

183

me to hating everything about me. It was awful. I felt lower than dirt.

"I remember one thing John said in particular that was really odd. I was talking about a friend of mine, and I mentioned how this person's ability to really listen to people was her forte [pronounced 'fortay']. John interrupted me and said, 'You're not saying that right, that's not how you pronounce forte. It's incorrect to pronounce the last 'e'. You should pronounce it fort.' 'Yeah, OK,' I said, brushing his comment aside, wanting to go on, 'the point is Jane is amazing how she can tune in to people and genuinely let in what they have to say.' 'No, Mary,' John replied, 'the point is if you're not going to communicate correctly, it's not worth communicating.' 'Huh?' I asked, confused. 'I just told you,' John sighed, talking in that falsely patient voice people use with children sometimes, 'forte is not pronounced fortay, it's pronounced fort.' 'But everybody says forte [pronounced 'fortay'],' I replied, tossing it off. It didn't seem important to me. 'Everybody?' John shot back. 'I see.' He shook his head, 'You're so dumb, Mary. I don't know why I bother trying to help you,' and he got up and walked out of the room.

"I was stunned. I felt shamed somehow, like there was something horribly wrong with me. John had never spoken to me like that before. It wasn't that he corrected my pronunciation—I'm no scholar—it was the way he did it. I looked up the word in the dictionary, later. Sure enough, there were two pronunciations, the one I'd heard all my life, 'fortay,' and his version, 'fort.' So after that, if I ever used the word in front of him I said 'fort.' But I felt so strange about it. I started watching my words, being real careful how I talked. It made me stutter sometimes, and John would just stare at me and finally say in an exasperated tone of voice, 'Spit it out already, Mary, I haven't got all day.'"

Mary shook her head, ruefully. She then continued, saying, "His words hurt so bad sometimes. I remember once I'd picked up our clothes from the cleaners. John was very particular about how he liked his shirts done. If they weren't done just right, he'd take them back two and three times. Or rather, I'd take them back two or three times. The same shirt. Anyway, I brought the clothes home and John took one look at a shirt, turned to me and said, 'Can't you do anything right? You're so stupid, Mary. I ask you to do a simple thing, like tell the cleaners to use light starch on the blue shirts, and medium starch on the white shirts. Look at this, this is ridiculous!' he says, tossing the shirts down on the bed.

"I started to explain to him that the cleaners had told me they were using a different type of starch and that if he didn't like it they'd be happy to redo them for free, but I never got past the first couple of words. 'The cleaners said . . .,' I started, and he interrupted me, 'Oh please, Mary. Now it's going to be the cleaner's fault?' I started again to explain, 'But . . .' and got no further. Shaking his head, John sighed, 'When are you going to learn to accept responsibility? I'm tired. You wear me out. Get rid of this stuff. I'm going to bed.' And off he went into the bathroom to get ready for bed. I sat down on the bed and cried."

BEDROOM ATTACKS

"Yeah," Bob said in reply to my question, "Karen started doing a number of things in addition to blaming me for most everything that was hurtful. I'd say the thing that got to me most was her verbal attacks." "Verbal attacks?" I asked, wanting to explore the issue. "Well, that may not be the psychological term for it," Bob said, "but that's what they felt like, so that's what I called them." "Tell me about them," I said.

Bob nodded, then said: "One of Karen's favorite areas of attack was the bedroom. I had not had much sexual experience. I had married young and been faithful to my wife until our divorce. After the divorce, I only slept with one other woman, and that was a brief three-week affair. My confidence in myself as a sexual partner was not the greatest. As a matter of fact, one of the reasons I was so entranced by Karen at the beginning was how she praised my sexual prowess. She really made me feel great, like I was the lover I always wanted to be.

"Oh man, did that change. Karen got real selfish in bed. If she was in the mood, I'd better be in the mood. You didn't say to Karen 'I'm sorry, honey I'm really bushed tonight, can I take a raincheck?' I tried that once, and what I got was 'You're just a selfish prick. You're not too tired to sit up and read, but if I want a little attention and affection, forget it. I hate you. Make love to your fucking book and see if that gets you off.' 'That's not true!' I said. 'I love you, I'm just tired, honey, I—.' But she cut me off. She didn't want to hear about it. She started yelling at how she was never too tired for me, how I never thought of her needs, it was always me, me, me. And on and on. It was no use trying to explain to her that making love took energy in a way reading did not or anything else. She hadn't gotten what she wanted and that was that.

"I'd run out of words, Dr. Noelle," Bob said, "I'd get so I didn't know what else to say. When things like this would happen I'd want to leave, but then I'd remember how good it could be with her when she was 'in the mood'—and not just sexually, but in general. When Karen was in a good mood, she was incredible to be with—fun, passionate, flirty, a real treat. And so I stayed." Bob was silent for a moment.

"But what she would say in bed that really hurt," Bob continued, rousing himself, "were things that had to do with my actual sexual performance. We'd be making love and suddenly she'd stop and say, in this irritated voice

'This is just not working for me, and I'd say, 'What would you like me to do, honey?' And she'd push me off her, or away from her, look at me, and say, 'If you were half a man, you'd know what I want. You're such a wimp. I can't believe I ever married you,' and she'd be on her way out of the bed, flipping on the TV or something. I'd say, 'Wait, don't go, come back honey, we'll try something else.' She wouldn't even listen, she'd be halfway down the hall yelling 'Go rent a porno—see if you can learn something. God. You're just pathetic.' I'd feel so ashamed, so humiliated. I did rent pornos. But that didn't seem to help much. You see, I could never figure out exactly what it was she might want on a given night, it was real hit and miss, and whenever I got it wrong, which was fairly often, she'd call me a wimp, stupid, a sexual moron, all sorts of names that made me feel lower than dirt."

Bob was quiet for a moment. "Was that the only area she attacked you verbally on, sex?" I asked. "No," he answered, "she had her other favorites." Bob sighed. "Karen rarely let an opportunity go by to harp on my more intellectual tastes and preferences. If I wanted to watch a science program and Karen wanted to watch a sitcom, there was no discussion about it. Karen would just launch into 'I'm sick and tired of your stupid intellectual bullshit! Who gives a damn about how many stars there are in a galaxy? And if I hear one more overdone voice caterwauling what you call opera I'll start yodeling. Sounds about the same to me. You are so pretentious—why can't you watch sitcoms like everybody else? Nooo—"Seinfeld" isn't good enough for you, you have to watch "Nova" or "National Geographic." Didn't you get enough of naked tribal tits when you were a boy? You make me puke.' She made everything I loved ugly. Like that comment about naked tribal tits. "National Geographic" is mostly about animals, for heaven's sake. It got so I didn't watch the programs or listen to the music I enjoyed any more. She made it so unpleasant when she didn't get her way, it just wasn't worth it."

Bob got up from the couch and paced as he continued to talk. "We differed in a lot of ways, Dr. Noelle. I tend to be neat and orderly, Karen likes to throw things around and wouldn't mind if there were piles of clothes, dishes, whatever, lying around everywhere. I'd put things away, not her personal things, but usually whatever was lying around in the kitchen or living room, like dishes and magazines. I'd hang up her sweater or coat from where she'd leave it lying on the couch. Karen would come roaring into wherever I was, and yell 'What the fuck did you do with my coat?' 'I hung it up in the coat closet in the front hall,' I'd say, and she'd come back with 'You are so prissy. You have to have everything all neat and nice all the time. Can't even leave my goddamn coat out overnight! It's like living in a sterile laboratory. No wonder you're such a lousy lover!' and off she'd stomp, throwing whatever was in her way at the wall, to get her coat.

"I'd stand there, sickened by her last comment. She rarely missed an opportunity to get something in about my lousy sexual abilities. Calling my preference for neatness sterile, calling me prissy, all these things hurt. So I learned to live in a messy house." Bob came back over to the couch and sat down.

"I'll tell ya, Dr. Noelle," Bob said, "I could close my eyes to the mess a heck of lot more easily than I could close my heart to the hurt."

CUTTING YOU DOWN

I asked Peter if Tony said hurtful things to him. "You mean outside of when we were arguing?" he asked. "Yes, was Tony critical of you or your life, for example?" I replied. Peter thought for a moment, then looked up at me, "Critical? Not directly. Not as in telling me I was ugly or something like that. It was more like he would put me down a lot." "Like how?" I asked. "Now how did I know you were going ask that," Peter said, grinning. I didn't respond, I just waited.

Finally Peter said, "OK, so this is get serious time. All right. Well, I had worked for this company for over six years, and they went out of business. It was really sad. This was a small family-run concern, good people, and even if it wasn't the best pay in the world, I'd enjoyed working there. I hadn't been out on the job market for a long time and I was anxious.

"I'd really look forward to Tony coming home to tell him of whatever job interviews I'd been on that day, what had happened. I guess I was needier than usual. So he'd come home and after saying hi and how are you and all that I'd tell him my day. He'd just say 'Uh-huh, that's great,' with that expression people have when they're really not interested and they just want you to get on with it. He'd continue with 'Now, wait until you hear what happened to me today.' And that was that. We'd spend the rest of the evening talking about Tony. I'd feel so let down. And yet there was nothing I could pin it on. He hadn't said anything mean to me. He hadn't said anything at all.

"I already felt down enough about being out of work. Tony would make me even more depressed by saying things like 'You didn't hear back from that interview Monday? Well, what do you expect. With all those qualified people out there, somebody like you didn't have much of a chance on that one. Cheer up—you'll get something!' He meant the comment to be supportive, at least that's what I thought he meant. But I didn't feel supported. The cheer up didn't cheer me up. I felt like there was a dig in there, something hurtful even though I couldn't pinpoint it. It was strange.

"When I did finally get a new job, after about two months of looking, it was a good job, better paying and with a company which provided more opportunities for personal growth and career development than had been available through my previous job. I was real excited, I could barely wait to get off the phone to tell Tony about it. All Tony had to say, though, as he sat there with the morning paper, never really lifting his eyes from the article he was reading, in a real condescending tone of voice, was 'Well, it's about time. I've never heard of the company, but I'm sure they're good. One can always hope.' I felt totally deflated. All the fun and excitement and eager anticipation of the new job just went pffft out of me, like air out of a balloon. Once again, Tony hadn't said anything deliberate to hurt me, but I felt awful, and I just about had to drag myself off to my first day at the new job.

"It got so I was real careful what I would tell Tony about. If something good happened at work, more often than not, I wouldn't tell Tony about it. He'd just put a downer on it, in one way or another. I found that things went better if we talked mostly about him or about things that weren't that special to me. It was easier that way."

PLEASURE DESTROYED

Teri laughed, "Critical? Anne criticized my every waking breath right from the start! How I dressed, who I saw, how I walked, everything. Only in the beginning she was very nice about it and always made me feel like she was just bringing out the best in me. It seemed I could do no wrong. Later that changed." "How did it change, Teri?" I asked. "Well," Teri said, "I guess she just stopped being nice about it." I looked quizzically at her, "For example?"

"For example," Teri said, "if I brought something home Anne approved of, all was well, she was really nice. But if I made the mistake of buying something she didn't approve of, even if it had nothing to do with her, she'd not only let me know it, she'd virtually annihilate my pleasure in buying the thing. Even when she knew how much it meant to me." Teri took a deep breath, then continued.

"I'd come from a small town, and I didn't have a car. I relied on public transport, which is OK, but . . . So when I had put aside enough money to buy a car, I was overjoyed. I'd combed the papers for good deals, asked around, tried to educate myself. Anne didn't pay much attention to my search. In her opinion if it wasn't a BMW or a Porsche, it wasn't. The fact that her BMW was 12 years old and creaking was irrelevant. It was a BMW.

"Well, I found a five-year-old single-owner Honda at a price I could afford, and made the deal. I drove it home, all proud, my first car! All excited, I ran in to tell Anne, and she came reluctantly outside to see it, saying 'It's cold out, why can't I see it tomorrow, when I have to go outside anyway?' but I didn't care, I made her put on her coat and she grudgingly came outside. She stood staring at my sweet little Honda, walked around it with a baleful look, sighed and said, 'So this is what you've been going on about.' She sighed again, 'Does it run?' 'Of course it runs, Anne, I drove it here.' 'Umhm,' she said, looking at it as if it were a sick cow. 'How much did you pay for it?' I told her, and she laughed and said 'Boy did you get had!' 'No,' I said, 'that's below blue book. It's a good deal.' 'Says who,' she asked, 'the previous owner?' laughing at her own joke. 'No,' I said, 'the mechanic I had look over the car.' 'Oh,' Anne said, 'Well— they're all crooks.' By now, my enthusiasm for showing her the car was down the toilet. Anne circled the car once more, sighed, and said, 'Well, maybe it'll last a couple of months.' She started to walk back into the apartment, and said mostly to herself, but loudly enough that I could hear, 'horrible color.' By then, I was so depressed I barely made it up the walk. I looked glumly at my to-me-new car that only a few short moments ago had brought me such joy. I tell you, Anne could take the fizz out of champagne. She sure as heck could take the joy out of me."

Case Analysis

In the development of a violent domestic relationship there is a predictable sequence: The physical violence that is to come later in the relationship is always preceded by other types of hurtful behaviors. The most common is verbal abuse. Verbal abuse comes in all shapes and sizes, from the most easily recognizable insults of the "bitch/bastard" variety to indirect criticisms and put-downs of everything about you. Most of us have no trouble recognizing verbal abuse when it comes in the form of a direct insult. Recognizing verbal abuse when it comes in the form of criticism and words that hurt is another matter.

POINTING OUT HOW YOU ARE STUPID, INEPT, AND DUMB

You're still in the glow of the wonderful beginning of the relationship. Sure, your partner tends to blame you for a lot of things, but heck, maybe that's just a way to blow off steam. Besides, you know you're not perfect, and you certainly do your share of messing up. And there's still lots of times when your partner is oh so loving, bathing you in the attention and affection you've come to crave.

The first time your partner criticizes you, you're taken aback. As Mary said, it's not the criticism itself that is so hurtful, it's the way it's said. In a healthy relationship, partners point out each other's flaws in a caring manner. Abusers point out flaws in a demeaning manner.

For example, when John noticed what he believed was a mispronunciation, he could have lovingly brought it to Mary's attention by saying "You know, I think there's a more correct way to pronounce the word 'forte'," and then told her what it was. When she replied "But everybody says 'forte' [pronounced 'fortay']," John had any number of possible responses available to him. He could have said, "I know, it certainly is the more common way," or "Well, you do have a point there," or "I don't think most people know the correct way of saying it." Any of these responses would have acknowledged Mary's reply without demeaning her. Mary laughed, "John would never say any of those. It just wasn't his style."

"My Way or the Highway"

If there's a style to how abusers do things, it could be called "my way or the highway." The constant theme underlying how abusers operate in a relationship is power and control: power over and control of their partner. When Mary opposed John's view of how to pronounce forte, she was being her own person, resisting John's control of how she spoke. To abusers, this is unacceptable. To reestablish his power over her, John immediately abused Mary verbally with "stupid" and "why do I bother," both said to put Mary back in a place from which she could be more easily controlled. When Mary said she felt like she'd been slapped, she was very accurately reflecting what John had done to her, albeit nonphysically: John had slapped her and, more specifically, slapped her down.

But why, you ask yourself, would anyone listen to such abuse? People listen because the abuse is camouflaged as criticism, and since most people want to please their partner they take that criticism to heart. "I loved him," said Mary. "I wanted to be wonderful for him, I wanted to be everything he wanted me to be. It felt very natural to try to fix whatever he saw wrong about me. It's just that some of it felt so unfixable." "What do you mean, Mary?" I asked. "Well, like the incident I told you about when I brought his shirts back from the cleaners," Mary replied, "I couldn't fix that, he wouldn't listen to me so I could explain what had happened."

Lack of Mutual Problem-Solving

Mary had a good point. Abusers don't listen to others. They are not interested in your point of view, because they are not interested in mutual problem-solving. Mutual problem-solving, which is crucial to a healthy relationship, is virtually impossible for abusive individuals. Either they have never learned how to do so successfully when growing up, or they do not trust the process. Either way, abusers rarely engage in interactive problem-solving with a partner. Abusers tend to solve problems either by giving orders, expecting those orders to be obeyed, and enforcing them with some kind of abuse when they're not, or by taking what they want.

Abusers expect you to behave like their shoe, an analogy I keep coming back to because it is so accurate. You want to go to the store, you put your shoes on and you go. You don't want to hear from your shoes that there's some reason they can't be worn that day. Abusive individuals want what they want when they want it. If you're not giving to them, they immediately seek to reinstate their power over and control of you. A quick and effective way to regain control is to weaken you by attacking you in an area in which you are already quite vulnerable.

PUTTING YOU DOWN WHERE IT HURTS MOST

"One of the things I really cherished about Karen in the beginning," Bob said, "was how special she made our sex life. It wasn't just how passionate and accomplished she was in that area, it was also how she made me feel like I was a real stud. I was so proud of how good she told me I made her feel in bed! Somehow I felt like more of a man. I know that's not a very nineties sentiment, Doc," Bob said, "but that's how she made me feel. So when she started to put me down in bed, that really hurt."

"I'm sure it did, Bob," I said, "but when would she put you down? Under what circumstances?" He thought about it for a moment, and said, "When she didn't get what she wanted." "Right," I said. "So maybe her putting your sexual abilities down had less to do with those abilities and more to do with her not getting what she wanted when she wanted it." "Go on," said Bob, intrigued. "When Karen would tell you, in the middle of love-making, that it wasn't working for her, you would ask her what she'd like you to do, correct?" I asked. "Yeah," Bob said, "and she'd never tell me. She'd just get out of bed, leave, basically." "So you never had an opportunity to put your abilities to work, did you? As soon as she let you know she was unsatisfied, she left. How were you supposed to satisfy her then?" "I don't know," Bob said, "I never thought about it that way." "Maybe Karen, not getting what she wanted when she wanted it, was less interested in working with you so she could be satisfied, and more interested in punishing you for not performing on cue," I said. "Huh," Bob said, "so we're back to power and control." "Yes," I said, "we are."

Punishing You for Getting Out of Line

When you're in a close relationship, be that an intimate relationship or a friendship, you find out all about the other person, what means a lot to him, where he is vulnerable, what his weak spots are. This is just as true of an abusive relationship as of a healthy one. When abusers want to punish you for getting "out of line," as it were, not behaving in the manner they expect, it only makes sense for them to aim directly at your vulnerabilities. It's more effective. The fact that they are in the process of causing you great pain is of no concern to them at that time. As far as abusers are concerned, you asked for it.

"So it would be the same when it came to my preference for certain TV shows and music and being neat and all that, right?" Bob asked. "Karen's putting me down for liking opera and reading and everything really wasn't about those things?" "Well, it was about those things to the extent that Karen had different tastes and preferences," I said, "but it doesn't sound like Karen was trying to negotiate a life together that had room for both of your tastes." Bob laughed, "No, she certainly was not."

"From your description, Bob, it sounds like Karen would verbally attack something valuable to you, like your reading or watching "National Geographic" when it got in the way of something she wanted," I said. "Does that sound accurate?" Bob stared at the floor, thinking hard. "Yes, yes it does, because if she was doing something else, like talking on the phone or painting her nails, she couldn't care less what I was doing. Heck, I could read or listen to opera, or whatever, she didn't object. It was only if she wanted something different that she would light into me."

Never Getting It Right

Since abuse is a power and control mechanism, it is used when the passive partner is seen as in some way escaping or rebelling against the abuser's power and control. This helps explain the unpredictability characteristic of the abuser's behavior. The abuser's definition of what constitutes escape or rebellion is often so personal and subjective that it is virtually impossible to predict the onset of abuse in many cases. (Certain behaviors, of course, are highly predictive of the onset of abuse, such as threats of leaving.) Not only do abusers define escape/ rebellion in a highly personal fashion, they are also hypervigilant in this regard, always looking to see if the partner is trying to elude their control. "It seemed like I could never get it right," Bob said. "No matter how hard I tried to please Karen, do things the way she wanted, pay attention to avoid what she didn't like, there was always something else I did that she didn't like and she'd start in on me again. I felt bad for letting her down and hurt by her verbal attacks. It felt like a losing battle."

Whoever coined the phrase "Sticks and stones may break my bones, but words will never hurt me" never lived with an abuser. Words hurt.

BEATING YOU DOWN WHEN YOU'RE UP

You're so excited, something wonderful just happened, and who do you want to share it with most? Your loved one or best friend, of course. You run home to tell her all about it and—nothing. Your partner either ignores your news, switches the subject to herself, or starts to tell you what's wrong with the wonderful thing that happened to you today. Within a matter of minutes, the happy excited feeling you had has turned to dust, or worse. You're let down, unhappy, depressed. Welcome to life with an abuser!

It's not that abusive partners don't want to see you happy. Oddly enough, that's not it at all. Abusive partners are perfectly willing to see you happy, as long as they and they alone are the source of that happiness.

The Abuser's Insecurity

Abusers are insecure people, frightened by the loss of love and desperately afraid that the loss of love is imminent. If something or someone else makes you happy, abusers fear that you will leave. Not knowing how to keep you by loving you more, abusers respond by trying to secure your affections in the only way they know how, tearing down or getting rid of anything that competes for your attention or affection.

Tony did not inquire about how Peter's job interviews were going; that might mean too much attention taken off Tony. He could not celebrate Peter's getting a job; what if that job meant Peter would have less attention available for Tony? Much of abusers' lack of supportiveness of their partner's lives is easy to understand, seen in this light.

Anne could not celebrate Teri's new car, since she'd had no part in the finding or the buying of it. The fact that she didn't choose to help Teri get the car is irrelevant. But since Anne was not involved, she could not approve of Teri's choice. Approval would have meant she supported something Teri did on her own, and the last thing abusers want is their partners out there doing something on their own. They might leave. So Anne proceeded to try to show Teri how her solo choice was a poor one. Again, it's not that abusers want to see you unhappy, just that they want to keep you in your place, with them. It's their way of reminding you that you are a lowly worm, basically inept and incapable, lucky to have someone as wonderful as them love you.

Your Success Is Not Your Own

Another tactic abusers use to devalue your accomplishments is what I think of as "possessing" the success of the other. For example, if you get a promotion or bonus from your place of employment, abusers will say it was because of their ideas, efforts, and supportiveness that you got the promotion. If you develop a new friendship, abusers will seek to become that person's friend as well. Whatever you accomplish or create, abusers will take credit for. One way or the other, either by destroying the value of the person/thing that makes you happy or by taking it over as "theirs," abusers see to it that your attention and affection remain focused on them.

Regardless of whether abusers trash your accomplishments in order to make you unhappy or not, the result is the same—you are unhappy. Eventually, like Peter, you stop sharing with your partner the experiences and people that are meaningful to you. It's just too painful to have your happinesses dragged down continually, especially by the person you most expect to be appreciative and supportive of you. Abusers are very good at destroying good feelings, first with words, later with fists.

TWELVE

How to Stand Up to Words that Hurt

YOU ARE TOLD YOU ARE STUPID, INEPT, AND DUMB

In the very beginning, your every word is precious to the abuser, your every action a source of delight. Soon enough that will change, usually within the first three months of the relationship. Abusers can find incredible fault with the tiniest aspect of how you walk and talk, how you dress, the pores on your face, the pound you gained.

Criticism

Criticism is not necessarily bad. Criticism, given in a constructive and loving way, can help us see ourselves as others do and gives us the opportunity to grow and develop. Constructive criticism is not demeaning. People who give you constructive criticism are genuinely interested in your well-being, and their comments are not demeaning. Constructive criticism generally includes suggestions for how to grow and develop and always respects your right to take it or leave it.

Criticism proffered by an abusive individual is a control mechanism. Abusive individuals will not offer criticism with alternative suggestions, but will issue orders or simply verbalize the criticism and leave it at that. The criticism is not meant to help you grow and develop in a way you choose; it is meant to control you, either by keeping you in your place (low side of pedestal) or by getting you to behave according to the abusive individual's wishes.

Helpful versus Hurtful Criticism

It's important to be able to distinguish which kind of criticism is being given to you. Just because your friend criticizes you doesn't mean the relationship is doomed to becoming abusive. "That sounds great," you say, "but how do I do it? 'You've gained some weight' sounds the same to me no matter whose mouth it comes out of!" Yes, it does, so it's important to follow up such a comment in a way that allows you to figure out whether the criticism is helpful or hurtful.

For example, you could follow up "You've gained some weight" with an acknowledgment (assuming the statement is true) and a request for more information: "Yes I have, any reason you mention it?" If your friend replies, "Well, I know sometimes you gain weight when you're upset and I wondered if there's anything going on with you," the criticism is constructive. If your friend says "No, just noticing" in a neutral or kind voice, the criticism is benign. You may not like hearing it, but you've not been abused.

If, however, your friend comes back with "Yeah, you look awful," you've just been criticized destructively. There is nothing helpful in telling you that you look awful. The statement is demeaning and hurtful.

Don't Accept Hurtful Criticism

Stand up for yourself. The first time a person says something critical about how you present or express yourself, let him or her know this is you and you like you this way. "How?" you ask. Verbal abuse, like physical abuse, unsteadies you. So first, take a deep breath; that will calm and center you. Then draw yourself up so you are standing (or sitting) tall, look your friend directly in the eye, and say in a calm, firm voice, "Please don't talk to me that way. There is nothing helpful in telling me I look awful." If your friend replies, "I'm just telling you for your own good," don't allow yourself to get side-tracked (a distracting maneuver). No matter what someone is trying to get across to you, saying it to you in a demeaning way isn't beneficial. Say, "Telling me I look awful doesn't feel good. I don't like it." If your friend replies, "You are so sensitive, I can't say anything to you without your getting all huffy or upset," stand your ground, take another deep breath and reply, "My being sensitive has nothing to do with this. Please don't talk to me that way, I don't like it." If your friend is a nonabusive individual, she will learn from this interaction how you prefer to be spoken to and will respect that from then on. You may have to point out your preference again on a couple of occasions, but your friend will clearly demonstrate her willingness to speak to you in a way that honors you by doing so most of the time.

For abusive individuals, this conversation won't make a dent in their behavior, other than to give them more fuel with which to criticize you: "You can't remember a damn thing, you're really slipping," they say contemptuously. Or "Oh, that's right, I forgot. I'm not supposed to say anything to Ms. Sensitive here—sorry."

The "Too Sensitive" Excuse

Abusive individuals frequently accuse their partners of being too sensitive, as if it were some character defect they should try to remedy. Passive partners, often aware that they experience pain—the world's as well as their own—perhaps more than other people, take such comments to heart and try to become more resilient to the active partner's verbal abuse. When you do this, you help your abusive partner abuse you! Someone who accuses you of being too sensitive is usually trying to justify their insensitive way of saying or doing things. Don't buy into the manipulation. You are who you are. You have the right to be spoken to in a way that feels good to you. Ask for it clearly and nondefensively: "Whether I am too sensitive or not isn't the issue. Please don't talk to me that way. I don't like it." Then watch what happens.

If your friend respects your request, she is probably not an abusive individual. If she doesn't, then you are in for more verbal abuse. Constant criticism, even if it's just a small and steady trickle, erodes self-esteem. Ask yourself, "Do I want to allow this kind of damage to myself?"

Accept Only Those Changes You Want for Yourself

Don't fall into the trap of revamping yourself to suit your friend's tastes. You are who you are and you are good enough as you are. "But Dr. Noelle," you cry, "I really do look awful, I've gained weight, I don't work out,

I'm tired all the time, the bags under my eyes are turning into suitcases, she's right!" Maybe so. If you decide that your friend's criticism points out something you want to change for yourself, so be it. But as with anything else you change in line with another person's wishes, be sure that change is something you would want for yourself whether or not that person remains in your life. Even when you agree with your friend's criticism, it's important for your self-esteem to tell her to bring the matter to your attention in a more supportive and constructive way.

Never Good Enough

Abusive individuals are fault-finders. Unwilling to deal with their own imperfections, they are hypervigilant and always focused on yours. As soon as you "fix" one thing in accordance with their wishes, they will find something else for you to fix. This characteristic makes it that much more important for you to stand your ground and only accept and work with those criticisms that you agree with wholeheartedly. Be aware that once the criticism begins, abusive individuals will continue to find fault with you throughout the relationship, regardless of how much or how often you revamp yourself. From the moment you fail to fulfill one of an abuser's unrealistic expectations and fall off that pedestal, you will never be "good enough" again. Sure, there will be periods of calm between the periods of criticism, but don't allow yourself to be lulled into thinking, "OK, I finally did it, I'm good enough for her." You will be simply deluding yourself.

Just as you cannot *be* good enough for an abuser, you can never *do* anything good enough for an abuser. Abusive individuals usually want things done a very specific and precise way, not because they are more evolved or somehow "better" than others, but because it provides them with yet another area of control. Even when you know this, and try to do things in that specific and precise way, an abusive individual will criticize you. There will be something about how you did it that will be wrong no matter how hard you try to please.

Enjoy Being You

Be yourself. Do things the way you like to do them. Don't think your lover is somehow right, that she knows better than you do how you should go about things. She knows how to go about things *differently* than you do. If you like some of her approaches, certainly feel free to adopt them, but only if you genuinely like them.

Be accepting of yourself. You have your way and she has hers. It's that simple. Accommodate your lover's preferences to the degree that is comfortable for you and let the rest go. Don't bend over backwards to do things the way your lover wants you to do them. It's normal when you care about someone to want to do things in a way that pleases that person. With a nonabusive partner, this is very doable. If you do something not quite the way your nonabusive lover likes it, she will let you know in a nonthreatening, noncritical way, and that's that.

Your Way Is OK

Abusive individuals will insist and demand you go about this their way. Stand up for yourself, let them know that you go about things the way you do out of choice. Say, for example, "I appreciate you don't like the way I do the grocery shopping, but this is the way I shop. If you'd like, we can sit down and talk about a different way we can handle grocery shopping together. I'll be happy to, but as long as grocery shopping is part of my chores, this is the way I choose to do it." If your lover continues to criticize how you do what you do, ask yourself if it is healthy for you to live in such an environment.

Stay In Touch with Who You Are

When you are in a relationship where you are constantly being criticized, constantly being made wrong and belittled, you can become totally focused on your lover's feelings and lose touch with your own. Passive partners frequently find themselves in this position, continually trying to fix whatever displeases the abuser, never really succeeding, and always more concerned with how their lover is feeling than with how they are feeling. This is precisely what abusive individuals want— for their feelings, wants, needs, and preferences to be the only feelings, wants, needs, and preferences that matter in the relationship.

It is often difficult in the wonderful beginnings of an abusive relationship to see that this is where you are heading. One way to figure it out is to notice, right from the beginning, if you are honoring *your* feelings, wants, needs, and preferences as much as you are honoring those of your new lover. Pay attention, as the relationship progresses, to any shift in the attention given by yourself and by your lover to *your* feelings, wants, and needs. In a healthy relationship, the focus is shared, with each individual honoring their personal needs as well as the needs of each partner.

PUTTING YOU DOWN WHERE IT HURTS MOST

Abusive individuals have an almost uncanny ability to know exactly where you are the most vulnerable and aim their most brutal comments at those areas.

Don't Accept the Hurt

Once again, stand up for yourself. Be willing to let your lover know how you feel. Take a deep breath, get centered, and say, in a clear, strong voice: "That hurt. If there's something we need to talk about here, then let's talk. But please, don't talk to me like that. I don't like it." People certainly say hurtful things to one another even in the healthiest of relationships, but once the hurt is exposed, they are willing to deal with it. If your lover says "OK, I'm sorry. I was pissed. We can talk," then there's the potential for a good relationship here. You may not talk about your lover's reason for being angry and your hurt right then and there, but the opening has been made to talk. Mutual resolution is possible.

The Willingness to Work Things Through Together

If your lover says, "Look, I'm just trying to be honest with you. It's for your own good," don't let that sidetrack you from your feelings. Say something along the lines of: "Honesty doesn't have to be hurtful. If we have a problem here, then let's talk about it." Listen very carefully. If the response is something like: "Well you just need to take care of this, that's all," they are implying they have no part in this, you are wrong, you are to blame, and you are responsible for fixing the problem. That's not a relationship! There is nothing mutual or together about you doing all the problem-solving. If something affects both of you, then both of you need to share the responsibility of working it through.

Being told something is for your own good may be appropriate when you are a child, and your parent indeed has a better idea of what is good for you than you do. But by the time you are an adult (barring highly unusual circumstances), you are able to figure out what is for your own good even if you choose to ignore that much of the time. A put-down is never for your "good." A lover telling you that a put-down is for your own good is just trying to get your attention away from his meanness. Don't accept that. If the put-down has nothing to do with the other person, but is aimed at something you do on your own, say, "That hurt. If you don't like something I'm doing then let's talk about it, but don't talk to me like that, I don't like it." Anything less than a willingness to either talk about whatever it is or apologize is indicative of an abusive relationship.

Be Observant

Watch closely what your lover does from then on. Does he respect your clear request to not be put down in such a way? Or does he ignore your request and continue to put you down? If your lover ignores your request and you are willing to let that go, you are putting yourself at risk. His inability to respect your request not to be verbally abused can all too easily turn into an inability to respect your right not to be physically abused. Be aware. Be alert.

Country cousin to putting you down in your areas of greatest vulnerability is the abuser's talent for putting down your favorite things and people. Abusers can turn your delight in a hobby or person into ashes with just a few well-placed put-downs.

Your Preferences Are OK

Stand up for your preferences. Say, in a clear, strong voice, for example, "I like going to religious services. Please do not put down what I enjoy doing," or "I enjoy spending time with Jeff and Marta. Please do not put down who I enjoy seeing." Offer to talk about your preference with your lover, but do not accept the put-down. Most often, abusive individuals are simply trying to exercise their control over you and therefore will refuse to discuss the issue.

If your lover respects your requests, wonderful, there may be the potential for a genuine relationship here. If he does not, and continues to put down those things and people you like, ask yourself how much joy you get out of remaining in a relationship with someone who puts what and who you love down all the time.

BEATING YOU DOWN WHEN YOU'RE UP

Since abusers are great fault-finders, it's really natural for them to maximize mistakes and failures. Abusive individuals can do this endlessly, without ever tiring or running out of steam. They seem often to take some sort of perverse pleasure in pointing out your mistakes and failures. What such individuals are really doing, though, is controlling you, or attempting to control you. Making you think you're a terrible person is one way abusers get you to stay with them, even when they are treating you horribly. If your self-esteem plummets low enough, you may well accept your abusive lover's definition of you as a flawed and defective human being and begin to believe that you are lucky to be in this relationship, abusive as it might be.

Stopping the Negativity

Don't let this happen. Stop the negativity immediately. If your lover starts dwelling on a mistake you made, for example, amplifying it and talking about it at length, say in a calm, strong voice, "I am well aware of the mistake I made. Please don't talk about it any more." If your lover replies, "Oh, OK, sure," and then drops the subject, terrific, you've stopped the negativity and retained your self-respect. If, however, your lover says, "Well I'm not sure you really see what happened here, you really messed up. You could be in a lot of trouble. I mean, I'm only telling you this for your own good," be careful. You're still being assaulted with negativity, just of a different kind. Don't get lured into an argument about whether you really are aware of the mistake. Stop the negativity by repeating: "I am well aware of the mistake I made. Please don't talk about it any more."

Negativity *Is* a Big Deal

If your lover insists on talking about your mistake, pay attention to her lack of respect. Know that it is a serious warning. Ask yourself what you are doing in a relationship with someone who keeps beating you down. Don't think, "Oh, well, it's no big deal, I can take it." No you can't. Negativity leads to mental and emotional disturbances of all kinds, depression being one of the most common. You will feel the deleterious effects of negativity on your self-esteem, and you will inevitably suffer the emotional consequences.

Making You Feel Small

If abusers are good at maximizing your mistakes and failures, they're even more gifted at minimizing your accomplishments and successes. Abusive individuals, having little self-worth or belief in their own value, are frightened that if you realize how valuable and worthy you are, you won't want to stay with them. Part of how abusive individuals seek to control you and assure your continued presence in the relationship is by sabotaging as best they can your accomplishments and successes.

Don't allow the sabotage. Be true to your value. If your lover says of the important promotion you just received, "Oh that's just a cost of living raise, no biggie," don't accept the diminishing comment, correct it. Say: "No, this wasn't just the regular cost of living raise everybody gets, this was a totally unexpected bonus, given expressly because of my superior performance over the past six months." If your lover says, "Wow, that's fantastic, I had no idea!"—congratulations. You are involved with a supportive lover who was simply unaware of what the promotion meant until you informed him.

Sabotaging Your Good Feelings

If, however, your lover says, "Uh-huh, yeah well, it's nowhere near what we need. It barely comes up to the cost of living index," pay attention. Notice that you are not being supported. Resist the temptation to defend your promotion to your lover, "But it really is a terrific promotion," explaining the details of it. This only gives abusive individuals the opportunity to further grind you into the dust. Why would you put yourself in such a misery-inducing position? Simply restate your truth: "It is a good promotion and I'm happy with it." Stay strong.

"Well I don't want to make such a big deal out of it," you say. You don't have to make a big deal out of it. Just be aware of what's going on. Don't allow your lover to undercut your good feelings of success. Share your good news with those who will actively support your joy and amplify it. Do recognize, however, that if your lover continues to take away from your successes in this manner, she will probably seek to take away from you all things that elevate you and help you grow. Ask yourself why you would want to stay in such a non-nurturing emotional climate.

Have the Courage to Speak Your Truth

Passive partners often find it difficult to correct their lover's minimizing assessment. Generally speaking, passive partners have difficulty contradicting anything the lover says. Get over it. If you are in a relationship where you cannot correct your partner's misunderstanding or stand up for your accomplishments, your growth, and your successes, you are in an unhealthy relationship that is emotionally abusive and may well disintegrate into one that is physically abusive. You cannot find out if you are involved with a somewhat distracted and misinformed nonabusive individual or a controlling and possibly abusive individual unless you are willing to speak your truth.

WARNING SIGN #6

Insensitivity

THIRTEEN

Lack of Caring
for the Well-Being of Others

LIFE'S A BITCH AND THEN YOU DIE

"It's amazing how much it's helping me to get angry about John's behavior," Mary said, "realizing it just is not OK to treat people like that." "And that you don't have to stand there and take it," I said, following her line of thinking, "that you have ways to deal with being unfairly blamed." "Yes," Mary nodded, "that feels good." She sat a moment, thinking. "I remembered some other types of things John would say that were hurtful," Mary resumed, looking up at me. "They weren't aimed at me, but they bothered me." "All right," I said, "go for it."

"Once," Mary said, "there was one of those television magazine documentary specials on that was showing all the children dying in these refugee camps. It was horrible, those tiny bloated bellies, and encrusted eyes, and mothers wailing at the death of their babies, helpless to do anything but watch their children die. I was really upset, unhappy over such things happening, feeling hopeless and like there wasn't much I could do in the face of so much misery. John was reading the paper. I said to him, 'Isn't it awful, so many children dying, I wish we could do something to help them.' John glanced up from his paper at the TV and said, 'Yeah? Hey, I wouldn't sweat it, there's too many kids in the world anyway.' I thought it was just another macho type comment. I didn't like it, it made me nervous, but I kind of brushed it aside.'

"To tell you the truth, Dr. Noelle, I didn't want to think about it. I think I was afraid if I thought about it, I might see a side of John I really didn't want to know about." Mary sighed. "I should have thought about it. It wasn't like it was just a one-time thing. That was pretty much John's general response to anything bad that happened to other people.

"If we heard about a plane crash or a tornado somewhere on the news, John would say 'Hey, that's the way it is, babe. Life's a bitch and then you die.' If I told him about a friend's misfortune, he'd say 'Yeah, so?' like it didn't matter and he didn't care. I was troubled by his responses but I didn't want to make a big deal out of them, so I kind of just let them go and didn't think about them." Mary stood up, troubled by her memories. She started to pace.

"I try to be socially conscious, you know?" Mary said, continuing, "I volunteer at an animal shelter once in a while, I support Greenpeace, I've worked with animal rights organizations, stuff like that—I do what I can, to help out in some way. I know a lot of people aren't interested in that sort of thing, so I tend to keep my interests to myself. But John was my love, my everything, so of course I told him. Well, John thought I was a real idiot for caring about animal rights and the environment. He would say things like, 'The environment doesn't care about you, why should you care about it?' or 'There's more animals than we know what to do with, Mary, so what if a couple of dolphins get caught in a tuna net, they're gonna die anyway, aren't they?' I didn't have good comebacks for those kinds of comments, so I'd just get quiet. All I knew was it made me real uncomfortable when he would talk like that."

KAREN AND HER DOGS

When I asked Bob if Karen had ever evidenced an uncaring or unfeeling attitude toward animals, the environment, or people in general, Bob sat and thought for a moment. Finally, he said, with a worried face, "Yes. I didn't know what to call it, it seemed wrong to me, that's how I used to think of it as, wrong, but uncaring, unfeeling? That would peg it just as well."

Bob stopped. He seemed agitated. "I hate talking about this," he blurted out. "We don't have to if you don't want to, Bob," I said, concerned. "No, it does help to talk about it—I just hate thinking about it," Bob replied. He sighed, then started: "Karen had two dogs. When she came to live with me in my house, she would let the dogs run free throughout the house. Well, they weren't trained. They would poop and pee everywhere, and chew everything. So I built a nice doghouse out back, with an old carpet tacked down inside and made it snug and warm. I fenced in a run, poured concrete down so it would be clean, and set her dogs up in their very own protected safe, clean area. That way they could romp and play and do whatever when we weren't at home and able to supervise them.

"Karen thought this was grand. But that was it. Karen would not take care of her dogs. She would forget to feed them, she wouldn't change their water for days on end, she wouldn't hose the run down, so they were running and slipping in their own poop, it was dreadful. She wouldn't groom them unless she was throwing a party, so most of the time they were all matted and dirty, and they smelled awful.

"I wasn't interested in dogs, that's why I'd never had any. Karen had agreed to take care of her dogs and knew I didn't want that responsibility. But when she'd fail to take care of them for days on end like that, the dogs were so pitiful, I couldn't not take care of them. Karen would say she was too busy, or the dogs didn't mind because they were used to her 'erratic schedule,' as she called it. Well they may have been used to it, but believe me, the dogs minded. I was there to hear them howl."

Bob stopped in his recitation for a moment, wiped his eyes, before continuing: "Oh I'm sure she did other things along the same line, but that's the one that really stands out. Those dogs."

Bob shook his head and was quiet for a while, then asked, "Do people's things count as 'the environment'?" "I'm not sure what you mean," I answered. "Well, Karen had this habit, this way of treating other people's things that seemed wrong to me. Kind of like the dogs—but not nearly as bad," Bob hastened to add. "Whenever we'd travel, even just get away for the weekend somewhere, Karen would trash anything that didn't belong to us. What I mean is, if we flew somewhere, she'd grab all the magazines on the whole plane for herself to read. She'd tear out whole magazine articles and anything else she was interested in, leave her seat area a real mess. If we rented a car at the airport, she'd trash the car. She'd drive too fast, not care if we ran over a curb, not care if she dropped ketchup on the seat or spilled soda on the dash. She'd make no attempt to clean anything up. She'd just leave used tissues and old food and anything she was done with all over the car.

"Same with the hotel room. She'd take whatever wasn't nailed down, and throw everything anywhere. The room always looked like World War III within an hour of our arriving. If I said anything about any of this, she'd accuse me of being uptight, of not knowing how to have fun. I don't know. I guess it just wasn't fun for me to trash stuff. I was very uncomfortable, but I didn't know what to do with the feelings."

A BIRD NAMED FRANK

When I asked Peter how Tony treated plants, animals, and the environment, he said, "Oh, boy, I haven't thought about that in a long time." "That what?" I asked. "The bird," Peter said, shaking his head, "Frank." "a bird named Frank?" I ventured, wondering if I got it right. "Yeah," Peter said, running his hands through his hair, "A bird named Frank."

"One day I came home and there was this enormous bird cage hanging from the middle of our living room ceiling. Inside the bird cage was a beautiful brilliantly colored parrot, a gorgeous blue, with bright black eyes, cracking open a seed of some kind. Tony came in from the bedroom with a big grin on his face and said 'How do you like him? I named him Frank after the one and only crooner. Wait 'til you hear him sing,' and he went up to the bird and started making noises at him.

"I was in shock and I was angry. We hadn't talked about this, but by now I was used to Tony making decisions that affected both of us without including me in the decision-making. I was also mad at this thing hanging right in the middle of the living room ceiling. I knew better than to say anything to Tony about it, but he saw the expression on my face and started to sweet talk me into accepting what he'd done, 'Oh, lover, don't be upset,'

Tony said, 'it's a lovely bird, and we'll be all the rage. Nobody else has one like him. And you'll see, they make great pets. We can teach him to stay on our shoulders and it'll be fun. Come one, give us a smile . . .' and he kissed and sweet talked and seduced me out of my anger, or at least to where I went, 'OK, OK, so we have a bird.' Tony promised to take care of it. 'You'll see,' he said. 'It's really easy, it's not like a dog or cat. All you have to do is keep the little bowls filled and change the paper in the bottom of the cage.'

"And he promptly proceeded to show me over the next couple of weeks how easy it was. Tony changed that paper every day, filled the little cups with water and seed, put the dark cloth over the birdcage at night, and whipped it off with a flourish in the morning. And everything the bird said was terrific in Tony's eyes, so we were one happy family.

"But after a couple of weeks, Tony got bored. He started to leave the paper in a few days. 'Frank doesn't poop that much,' Tony would say. Tony would forget to replenish the bird's water and seeds, and by the end of the third week would yell 'Oh shut up' when the bird would talk, and yell insults at the bird if it didn't get quiet immediately.

"After a month, Frank was one very depressed bird. His plumes lost their luster, his eyes their gleam, and he would alternately sound off until Tony would throw the dark cloth over the cage or refuse to say a word. I was relieved for myself, no doubt, but even much more so for the bird when Tony exclaimed 'I can't stand that thing— get it out of here!' I didn't say 'That's your responsibility, not mine.' I ignored that minor detail entirely and was very pleased to find a good home for Frank.

"I was so upset with what Tony had done. It's just not right. You can't take on an animal like that and not take care of it. It's not right."

Tony's Game

Later, Peter also talked about a game Tony loved to play, a game that made Peter highly uncomfortable. "You know the way Tony treated the bird? Well, I think Tony felt pretty much the same way about people as he did about Frank. They were expendable." "How do you mean, Peter?" I asked. "Tony had this game," Peter said. "He used to call it 'The Price is Right.' It went like this. Peter would say, 'There is this old man in India who is dying of old age, starvation, whatever. Now, regardless of what anyone does he is absolutely going to die. Let's say you could collect $100,000 if you push a button that would kill him, that no one would ever know what you did. Would you push that button?'

"Now most people would say no. Often they'd be kind of shocked that he asked such a thing. I know I was. And this is where the game began. Tony would say, 'OK. Would you do it for $500,000? $1,000,000?' And the person would still say no. Then Tony would start to point out what you could do with $1,000,000, and how the old man would never know, and actually you might be doing the old coot a favor, sparing him further misery, and on and on. I was horrified. Tony would get so passionate about this, so convincing, it was like watching a hawk going after a mouse, eyes glinting, single-minded focus. And if the person finally said yes, Tony would lean back, gloating, and say 'Everyone's got their price.' If the person didn't succumb he would just say 'Haven't found your price yet, I will.'

"I hated that game. Tony would play it with anyone new we met. Given that we used to go to the gay clubs a fair amount, we met a lot of people all the time. I didn't know why it made me so uncomfortable. Tony said I was just a sissy, a pie-eyed optimist who refused to see people as they are. Maybe so, all I know is I hated it."

ANNE'S BLACK THUMB

Teri spoke of Anne's poor treatment of her plants. "Anne used to joke about her 'black thumb.' That all she had to do was look at a plant and it would die. But what I realized, after a while, was that Anne was very erratic in how she took care of her plants.

"She fell in love with this giant ficus, for example, and brought it home. Here was this big tree in the living room now, and for a few days she was all happy about it. She would water it and spray the leaves and whatever else you're supposed to do with ficus. But after a little while, the leaves turned yellow and some fell off and the ficus looked sick. Anne's response was to get irritated and complain. 'How could it do this to me? Damn tree, here I watered it and took care of it and now it's dying on me. Stupid tree.'

"But the truth of it was, she hadn't paid attention to the kind of light a ficus needs, nor the appropriate watering and type of food a ficus needs. She'd just stuck it where it looked pretty and expected it to thrive. Once it got sickly, Anne didn't care about the plant any more and just cursed at it. So I went to a nursery, found out what you're supposed to do for a ficus, took it into my room, gave it the kind of sunlight and nutrients it needed, and nursed it back to health. Anne's only comment was 'Well can I help it if I'm cursed with a black thumb, Miss Green Thumb?'

"Anne was oblivious to my suggestions that if she's going to buy a plant, maybe it'd be a good idea to find out what that plant needs. The next time the urge struck her to buy a plant, Anne just bought whatever pleased her, and promptly proceeded to repeat the cycle. She'd fail to take care of the plant entirely, as if it were a plastic plant and could live on air, or water it obsessively the first week or so and then wonder why it was dying. She never stopped to consider what the plant needed."

Case Analysis

Abusers are angry people. They are not necessarily bad or evil, but they are angry people. However happy abusers may be at a given moment, underneath they have great storehouses of unexpressed anger. Much of the anger is repressed, which means they are not conscious of it.

EMPATHY

It is difficult to feel empathy when you are angry. Empathy is the capacity to put yourself in the place of others, to feel some of what they feel. Empathy is what makes genuine caring possible. You can *caretake* in the absence of empathy, which is to provide services for others, but you can't *care* for and about them in any real sense in the absence of empathy.

Lack of Empathy Leads to Cruelty

Webster's defines *cruel* as "disposed to inflicting suffering." The less empathy you feel toward others, the easier it is to inflict suffering. Abusers may or may not always intend to inflict suffering, but that is what they do. Long before abusers engage in physical violence against you, their disposition to do so shows up in other areas, for example, in their indifference to or willful neglect of the well-being of children, animals, and plants; their disregard or destruction of the property of others;

and typically, their callous attitude toward the suffering of others.

CALLOUS ATTITUDE TOWARD THE SUFFERING OF OTHERS

Behavior follows attitude and belief. If a person has a belief that human beings aren't worth much, then from the basis of that belief they can easily develop an uncaring attitude toward the fate of others. That attitude in turn makes it possible for that person to inflict suffering. After all, if people aren't worth much, what difference does it make if they suffer?

No matter how differently your new love or best friend may treat you in the wonderful beginning of the relationship, eventually abusers will treat you as they treat every one else, badly. People who are not attuned to and concerned with the well-being of others will not be attuned to and concerned with yours. Mary was right to feel nervous when John made repeated nonempathic comments about other people's suffering. They were indicative of a callous or uncaring attitude toward others' pain, a precursor to the infliction of pain. John already lacked empathy for the emotional distress he caused Mary, as seen in Chapter 7. In time, John would demonstrate the same lack of empathy toward the damage his physical violence would cause her.

How You Are Relatively Valued

Abusers are largely out of touch with their own value. Since they do not experience their own worth, it is difficult for them to value others. "But I've never felt so loved!" you object. "He values me tremendously." You may feel valued, but it would be more accurate to say that abusive individuals *expect* of you tremendously, and invest you with almost magical powers to fulfill them in a multitude of ways. As long as you are fulfilling their every expectation, abusers will accord you great value, certainly, but your value resides only in your ability to fulfill their needs. This may feel like love, but, as we will see, just because something feels like love doesn't mean it is love.

Tony's game, for example, shows a profound lack of appreciation for the value of human life. The avidity with which Tony played his game is an attempt to justify his callousness, as if to say "See, no one else really believes in the value of human life either; I'm just more honest about it." Peter's "hate"of the game is a good sign! Unfortunately, Peter did not see the game for the warning sign that it was, a callous attitude that made physical violence entirely possible.

INDIFFERENCE TO AND WILLFUL NEGLECT OF THE WELL-BEING OF CHILDREN, ANIMALS, AND PLANTS

People usually consider humans the most valuable life forms on the planet, followed by pets, other animals, plants, and then what is loosely termed the "environment." Failure to value any one of the nonhuman life forms or the environment lays the groundwork for failure to value the higher life forms, namely you.

When Mary talks about the uncomfortable feeling she had when John would comment in a disparaging way on her concern for the environment and animal rights, she is reflecting her innate awareness of the significance of John's attitude. Unfortunately, because John did nothing more than voice his opinion, Mary didn't pay much attention. She didn't stop to seriously consider what such an attitude might mean because, as Mary puts it, she was afraid she might see a side of John she didn't want to see. That's why passive partners often feel blindsided when the violence happens. The warning signs have been there all along, but they don't want to look at them. Passive partners don't want to find out that their relationship isn't the fairy tale they want it to be.

Ignoring Needs

You may pay a little more attention to someone's active neglect or failure to take care of a plant, but not much. Teri certainly didn't appreciate Anne's buying plants, letting them die, and then just buying more plants, but she never thought about what such a pattern might mean. "I knew it wasn't a very caring attitude," Teri said, "but these were just plants, Dr. Noelle, lots of people don't treat plants right." "That's true, Teri, and lots of people who don't treat plants right don't go on to abuse their loved ones," I said. "This isn't a one-to-one correspondence. What's significant about Anne's neglect of her plants was her failure to learn about or pay attention to the plant's needs." "Oh, I get it," said Teri. "If Anne could ignore the plant's needs, she could ignore mine." "Yes," I said, "it doesn't mean she would necessarily. It means it was within the realm of what is acceptable to Anne. We're talking about a warning sign, not an inevitability."

Neglect as a Violation

Since neglect does not involve hitting or striking, you may not see it for the violence that it is. But neglecting the needs of a pet, to the extent that the animal's well-being is endangered, is violence. An individual capable of mistreating a pet to that extent is fully capable of mistreating you in the same way. Bob found this out, to his great dismay. "The longer I was with her, the clearer it was that Karen didn't care about anybody except Karen. Oh, she'd say she loved me, and when she wanted to be, she was the most passionate woman I've every known. She wanted me to be there, for her, when she wanted me to be there. But that was about it. What I wanted, what was important to me, that didn't matter. She'd walk off and leave me hanging just like she left the dogs, howling, day in, day out."

In the absence of children around the house, abusers' cruelty shows up most often in their treatment of animals. Karen's neglect of her dogs is typical of how abusers relate to animals, as is Tony's neglect of his parrot. Tony treated the bird like a toy, not like a living thing. Once the novelty of having a parrot wore off, Tony effectively discarded the parrot, just as a child would a toy, refusing to take responsibility for attending to the parrot's well-being or finding it a better home. An individual who can in essence "throw away" an animal is perfectly capable of "throwing away" a human being.

DISREGARD OR DESTRUCTION OF THE PROPERTY OF OTHERS

We take so much of what people do at face value, we don't stop to think about the implications of their behavior. When people don't treat another person's possessions with respect, it's because they don't care about the impact their actions will have on that person. Thieves are capable of stealing because they don't care about the impact of their actions or because they care more about their well-being than about the well-being of the person from whom they are stealing. When people care about the impact of their actions and the well-being of the person involved, they are incapable of stealing. When you care about your impact, you will not mistreat another person's possessions deliberately.

Awareness of Impact

"I don't think it ever occurred to Karen to think about how other people were impacted by what she was doing," Bob said. "She just did what she wanted to do." "Did that bother you?" I asked. "Sure, it bothered me," Bob replied, "but I never thought about it in terms of what it meant to me." "The larger scope of things," I commented. "Yeah," Bob said, "I mean, I just thought, 'Oh, that's how Karen behaves to have fun, let off steam, that's her way of getting R&R—you know, rest and relaxation." People are consistent with themselves. People who are indifferent to how somebody is going to feel when he finds his possessions damaged are likely to be indifferent to how you will feel when you get damaged.

When people don't care about others' rights or their well-being, physical violence becomes an all too easy and readily acceptable response to any number of situations.

FOURTEEN

How to Recognize an Uncaring Attitude as a Precursor to Violence

A CALLOUS ATTITUDE TOWARD THE SUFFERING OF OTHERS

Abusers tend to be focused exclusively on themselves: their wants, their needs, their pains, their woes. Abusive individuals have little capacity for empathy, the ability to stand in another's shoes and feel what another feels. The pain and suffering of others in the world doesn't have much impact on abusers. Unfortunately, neither will yours.

Listening for the Callousness

A callous attitude toward the suffering of others is primarily revealed in conversation, in the comments some-one makes on the ongoing wars, diseases, and other disasters of our world. Listen up. If you hear your lover voicing an opinion that seems to reflect a callous attitude, take it seriously. We tend to dismiss a person's comments as just idle talk, yet people's behavior is sourced in how they think about things. Investigate your lover's thinking. Ask as neutrally as you can: "How did you come to such a conclusion?" or "What makes you think that?" You may find out much to your delight and surprise that your lover's comment comes from a well thought out philosophical or moral position that takes the suffering of people into account in a way you had not thought of. You may discover that in fact he cares very much about others' welfare. Your lover may, on the other hand, respond to your question with something along the lines of "Everybody knows that, what a dumb question," which tells you his comment indeed reflects his lack of empathy, not a carefully considered moral position.

Don't discount your lover's callousness. Don't pretend that it really isn't that important. Attitude paves the way for behavior. A person unconcerned by the harm inflicted on others is likely to be unconcerned by the harm inflicted on you.

Lack of Caring Is Rarely Just Ignorance

Passive partners frequently make the mistake of thinking that abusive individuals don't care about others because they just don't know any better. This may be true of an adolescent, but by the time we've reached adulthood, most of us have outgrown such self-centered ignorance. Don't try to convince a person of the need to care for others. If your lover isn't already aware of it, question why you would want to be in a relationship with this person.

INDIFFERENCE TO AND WILLFUL NEGLECT OF THE WELL-BEING OF CHILDREN, ANIMALS, AND PLANTS

It is one thing to be ignorant, it is another to be indifferent. To be ignorant of something is to be unaware of the problem or of the implications of the problem. Indifference is an attitude of noncaring: You know about the problem, but you don't care. When you are indifferent to the fate of the environment, for example, you don't care that our waters are polluted, the rainforests are being destroyed, or that the disposal of garbage has taken on epic proportions. It doesn't affect you personally, so you don't care.

Indifference

Abusive individuals tend to be indifferent toward whatever does not affect them directly. The environment is usually too "out there" to have immediate impact on people and can readily be ignored. "But Dr. Noelle," you say, "lots of people don't care about the environment." True, and lots of people aren't violent in their domestic relationships. However, indifference to the environment is indicative of an attitude that supports lack of caring in the face of distress—the earth's or yours.

Willful Neglect

Willful neglect goes much further than indifference or lack of caring. Willful neglect is when a person takes on the responsibility for the well-being of another person, animal, or plant and neglects those responsibilities knowingly. Willful neglect is abuse. The Department of Child Services, for example, defines it so with regard to children. Don't think it won't spread to you. The ability to willfully neglect the well-being of a child, pet, or plant is evidence of an underlying attitude of disregard for the well-being of others. Don't think your friend's willful neglect of a pet or plant is less important because these aren't human beings. How individuals treat their pets and plants is highly reflective of how they will treat the people in their lives.

Pay attention. Don't discount your friend's willful neglect of a pet or plant: "Oh, she's just too busy to take care of the animal" or "She just doesn't deal well with plants." If your friend is too busy to attend to the well-being of an animal, she has no business getting a pet, or she should look into getting help for the care of the animal. If someone doesn't deal well with plants, he or she can learn how or can buy plants that don't require much attention. What's important is to realize that such willful neglect fits into a larger pattern of disregard for others, which increases the potential for abuse.

DISREGARD OR DESTRUCTION OF THE PROPERTY OF OTHERS

Failure to respect the possessions and property of others is also indicative of a lack of concern for the well-being of people. An individual who feels she has the right to destroy or take another's property may feel entitled to do as she pleases in general, without regard for the impact of her actions. Keep your eyes open and stay alert to how your friend treats other people's things. It will tell you a lot about how she is capable of treating you.

WARNING SIGN #7

Past and Present Violence

FIFTEEN

The Alarm Goes Unheeded

PUSHED INTO A WALL

Mary was subdued when she came for her session that day. She took a moment to get comfortable on the couch, then looked at me and said, "I think I'm ready to talk about how the violence started." I nodded. I was pleased. I knew how much courage it had taken for Mary to get to this point. I also knew how critical it was for her further healing.

Mary started very simply: "John was very interested in sound systems. He had subscriptions to various magazines that described the latest in CD players and speakers and all sorts of stuff like that. John would go on and on about how certain German components were the best ever. He said German technology was so much more precise and rendered certain sounds better than any other, especially the Japanese, who might know how to make things cheap but they certainly didn't know how to make things right. He felt it was no big surprise, given the excellence of German automobile technology, that they were equally competent in the area of sound technology. I know nothing from nothing in this area so I would just nod and listen.

"Well, one night we were at dinner at a nice restaurant with another couple, a friend of mine from work and her husband, Bill. The men started talking about sound systems. Suddenly, here's John who has been praising German systems forever, who's totally agreeing with Bill about the wonderfulness of Japanese systems. Bill is saying how the Germans don't know what they're doing, and how much the Japanese are vastly superior in this area. John's saying 'Absolutely, the Germans are backward and positively prehistoric relative to the Japanese.' I'm puzzled. This is the exact reverse of what I had heard at home for the past year. I said to John, in a surprised tone of voice, 'But I thought you always said the Germans were superior when it came to sound,' and John shot me this nasty look, then laughed and said very pleasantly, 'Honey, I don't know where you came up with that,' and turned to Bill to continue the conversation.

"I was confused and puzzled, but thought no more of it, and we had a very nice evening, and drove home. Once we were home, I remember, I was hanging my coat up in the hall closet. John came close to me and said in this awful cold voice, 'You will never contradict me in public again. Never.' He turned and started to walk away, I said, 'What? What are you talking about?' He turned back to me and said, 'You contradicted me in front of Bill.' I remembered now what the conversation was and said, 'Oh, that. Well, you've been telling me for months about German systems.' 'You're doing it again,' John said, 'you're contradicting me,' and he started to walk toward me. I was completely not understanding and trying to sort it out when I realized he wasn't just walking toward me, he was walking me into the wall. We had a side table against the wall, I bumped into it as he walked forward into me. I fell down hard onto the tiled floor, cried out in pain. He just stood right there over me where I had fallen and said, 'You will never contradict me again,' in this awful voice. I was crying and saying, 'You hurt me, you hurt me,' but he just walked away. He walked into our bedroom, shut the door, and left me crying on the hall floor.

"I couldn't believe what had just happened. I would never in a million years have predicted John would do such a thing. Never.

"I was stunned. I was in such shock I somehow convinced myself that it wasn't John's fault. He had been taking pain pills for a back injury and I convinced myself it must have been a side effect of the pain pills. He couldn't possibly have been in his right mind.

"I limped to the bedroom and sat on the edge of the bed, where he was watching TV. I asked him, 'Are you still on those painkillers?' He nodded. I said, 'That's what it is, I'm sure of it. You would never have hurt me otherwise. I know you, that's just not like you. It has to be the painkillers, you didn't know what you were doing. I know you didn't.' He looked at me and his face softened, he took me in his arms and said, 'Thank you for understanding,' and held me tight and somehow I thought everything would be fine again. In my relief, I did not notice that he didn't say 'I'm sorry' or anything like that.

"The next night, when we were undressing for bed, he noticed the huge bruise I had on my hip and thigh from falling down. He said, 'What's that from?' I looked at him, surprised, 'From the fall—last night.' He said, 'Oh' very neutrally, and then said, 'You should be more careful where you're going, Mary, you could hurt yourself.' It was as if the incident had never happened. I was so confused. And somehow I felt like it was my fault. That if I was hurt, I was to blame. It was very strange.

"Now when I look back at it, I am so ashamed and humiliated that I did that—that I somehow excused John of being violent with me. But at the time, it seemed the natural thing to do. I was shocked, confused, and desperate. I couldn't accept, I just couldn't, that he deliberately on purpose would hurt me. But he would. And he did. The next time, though, I was ready for it.

"About a month later, when he started coming at me, I saw this look in his eyes and I just froze. I stopped talking, moving, breathing. He came all the way up to me, pushing against me, pushing me into the wall, practically spitting in my face as he told me how I had offended him. But I didn't fall down. And at least this time, I didn't seek to excuse him. This time I knew he had done it deliberately. The funny thing was, I still didn't think of what he had done as 'domestic violence.' After all, he hadn't lifted a hand against me. He hadn't hit me. I didn't make the connection until he did hit me."

A KICKER AND A THROWER

When Bob was ready to talk about Karen's violent behavior, he described it as follows: "Karen was a kicker and a thrower. If whatever the thing, person, or animal it was that had somehow displeased her was within kicking range, she kicked it. If it was too far away to kick, she threw things at it. I mean that literally. If the car wouldn't start, she'd kick it. If the dogs wouldn't come when she called, which was most of the time, she'd throw something at them. If the dogs didn't get out of her way fast enough, she'd kick them.

"What was strange, now in hindsight, was that I didn't see what she was doing as violent. I just thought of her as excitable and hot-tempered. It's not like she threw knives at the dogs. She'd throw a pillow or a paperback. Usually she'd kick the car tires, not the door. So I didn't realize quite what it meant until she started in on me.

"We were arguing about money, I don't recall what exactly, but we were often arguing about money. Karen never bothered to look to see if we had enough money before she'd buy something, so I was forever juggling bills and charge cards, and I would get mad at her. I was trying to get her to see how if we could just figure out a budget and stick to it, we'd be a lot better off. She was furious, yelling how I was a selfish prick, and how all I thought of was buying computer upgrades, and she should be able to buy what she wanted when she wanted without being accountable to me, and on and on.

"I tried to tell her it wasn't about being accountable to me, it was about being accountable to us, and she just got so furious she was tongue tied. She grabbed a heavy ashtray off the table and threw it full force at me. Fortunately, I ducked. The ashtray went sailing through the sliding glass door, missing me by inches. 'Now look what you've made me do!' Karen cried out, furiously, 'you bastard, you s.o.b.,' and on and on, as she proceeded to throw everything within her reach at me. Finally, spent, she fell to the floor and sat there crying, saying over and over how it was all my fault.

"Without realizing what was happening, I found myself consoling her, as if she was the one who had been damaged. And that became our pattern. Karen would get mad, start throwing things, sometimes hit me, sometimes miss me, end up crying, completely worn out, telling me it was all my fault. I'd end up consoling her, even if I was nursing a cut or bruise. Why I didn't see then that such behavior was domestic violence, I have no idea. I just kept saying to myself 'It's the downside, OK? She's a great lady, she's the most passionate woman you've ever met, so she has a hot temper, so what?' I had no idea what that 'temper' would lead to."

THE VIOLENCE OF JEALOUSY

Peter first talked about Tony's violent behavior in terms of Tony's jealousy: "Right from the beginning, Tony made it very clear that if he ever caught me cheating, he'd kill me. We'd be in the middle of making love and he'd say something like, 'I love your body so much, if I ever thought someone else's mouth had been here, I'd kill them,' then he'd draw back and look at me and say very slowly, very seductively, 'And I'd kill you too,' and then go back to making incredible love to me. It was tremendously exciting! I'd never been wanted that much. I equated Tony's jealousy with his love.

"If we were at a club, he'd tease me about how some good-looking guy was flirting with me (whether it was true or not) and then would whisper very sexily in my ear, 'You know what I'd do if I caught you two together?' and then he'd tell me graphically and in explicit detail which body parts he'd cut off of each of us and do what with. Now, I didn't particularly like this game, but Tony had this way of talking. When he was talking dirty that was such a turn-on, it hardly mattered. I was besotted with his voice, his way of talking, and virtually ignored what he was saying. I certainly never took his violent words and threats seriously.

"But then, one night we'd been out to a movie, actually, we were standing in line outside the theater, and a guy walked by, did a double take, and came back to me. 'Peter?' he said. I looked, and recognized him as a former lover—an affair, not a major relationship. 'It *is* you,' he said, 'My you're looking well.' 'Skip,' I said, 'how are you doing? This is my lover, Tony" introducing Tony. The man said hi to Tony, said it was good to see me, and left. We went in to the movie theater about then, saw the movie, and then left to come home.

"Tony was very quiet. As soon as we got home, the door barely shut behind us, Tony started in on me, 'Who was that?' 'A guy I knew once,' I said. 'A guy, just a guy, huh, Peter?' said Tony, warming up to it. 'Yes, Tony. A guy I had a brief fling with. OK? It's over, it's been over for years, I don't even know where he lives or anything else now,' I said. Tony eyed me, warily, 'But he sure knew how to find you.' I looked at him like he was nuts, 'Tony, we were standing in a movie theater line. He didn't find me as in track me down.' Well it didn't matter what I said, Tony was pissed. He started yelling at me that I was a cheating whore, that I was just looking for an opportunity to cheat on him and on and on. I could see this argument was going nowhere. Tony wasn't interested in hearing my side of it and I thought this was crazy. I grabbed my jacket off the sofa, and said 'I'm going for a walk,' and started walking toward the door.

"Tony grabbed me by the back of the neck so fast I thought I'd been hit by something. He twisted one arm up my back, and holding me like that, back of neck and arm, he almost whispered into my ear, in the coldest rage I'd ever heard, 'Don't you ever walk out on me. Ever.' We just stood there in complete silence, for what felt like the longest moment. He yanked up on my arm just once and I yelped. 'Do you hear me?' he asked. 'Ever.' I was absolutely terrified. No one had ever restrained me physically like that. When I could find words, I said, 'Yes, fine, I'll never walk out on you, ever.' Tony slowly let go of my arm, my neck, and then said, 'You belong to me, Peter, and you belong with me. Don't make me jealous. I can't handle it.'

"He left the room. I sat down on the sofa, shaking. I needed to think. Somehow something had gone very wrong. I didn't know how, and I didn't know what to do about it. I felt awful. But I knew Tony loved me and that I loved him. He was right, we did belong together. I was scared. I didn't want to get hurt again but I didn't want to leave him.

"Over the next few days I tried to sort it out. I finally convinced myself it wasn't so bad, it was just that Tony was really jealous. And wasn't jealousy proof that he truly loved me? I would see to it that I wouldn't do anything to get him jealous. That's how I thought I could handle it. I was so wrong."

SIBLING RIVALRY

Teri did not directly witness Anne's violent behavior, but the evidence of such behavior was there, in Anne's stories. "I can't believe I didn't connect it at the time," Teri said. "Anne was telling me, flat out, what she was capable of!" Teri shook her head, continuing, "Anne would talk about how she hated her older sister, Irene. How when they were girls together, Irene was the pretty one, Irene was the smart one, Irene was the popular one, and how Anne absolutely hated her for it. What made it worse was that they were only a year apart. So by the time they were in junior high and high school, Anne and Irene were often in activities together. They were with the same group of kids, and yet Irene was always the one being courted, invited, appreciated. Anne was the one sitting on the sidelines.

"Only Anne's way was not to just sit in the sidelines. Anne told me she would take every opportunity to get back at her sister for being so 'Miss Wonderful.' She would carefully unstitch seams in Irene's dresses, so that Irene's dresses would pull apart, embarrassing her in public places. Anne would arrange for 'moth holes' to appear in her sister's favorite sweaters or steal her sister's favorite lipstick. Anne would 'forget' to give her sister telephone messages, always went through her mail, and destroyed anything in there she thought Irene might value.

"And of course, Anne would tell me, they fought. According to Anne, Irene, being Miss Wonderful, would fight clean. Arguments, yelling, but no cuss words and no hitting or anything like that. Anne told me she herself had no such compunctions. Nasty words were fair play, and hitting was just the beginning. Anne pulled her sister's hair, clawed her face, rammed a pencil in her hand (the lead was still there to this day), sat on her back and pummeled her, and bit her sister's arms and legs any time she could get near them.

"Anne also bragged of shutting her sister up in a closet for hours on end, even though she knew her sister was claustrophobic and would suffer greatly from such confinement. Once Anne managed to shut Irene up in a room with a snake she'd found out in the garden. Irene was terrified for hours and walked around skittish for days thereafter, much to Anne's delight.

"There appeared to be no end to the ways Anne devised to make Irene suffer. As soon as Irene was on to one of her tricks, Anne would come up with another. Listening to these stories, I would laugh. Anne had a way of telling them that was very engaging, very funny. It was like reading *Huckleberry Finn* or something. I half believed her, half didn't, but it sure made a good story. I didn't stop to think about the impact of Anne's actions on Irene, the pain she must have caused her sister. All I saw at the time were funny stories, sibling rivalry, nothing to do with me.

"Only later, when I began to have my own set of friends, when I began to date, funny little things would happen. I wouldn't be able to find my eye liner the night of a date, or somehow my dress would be missing a button. I couldn't find books I'd borrowed from friends, and people would tell me they'd called only I never got the message. Nothing big, and Anne was always so sympathetic. I didn't even connect what was happening with the stories she'd told me about her and Irene. It wasn't until much later, when she killed my cat, that I remembered, all in a flood, her tales of violence towards Irene. I can't believe I didn't pay attention. I hadn't realized how what she did with Irene was violent. If I had, my cat would still be alive." Tears ran silently down Teri's face as she remembered the awful night Anne set fire to her belongings, "Burning up is such a terrible way to die."

Case Analysis

To the abuser, violence is an acceptable response to stress and frustration. It is part of a larger pattern of the abuser's use of power over and control of others as the primary way of interacting in personal relationships. It is well known in psychology that the best predictor of future violence is past or present violence. ***The use of force or any display of physical violence toward a partner in a relationship is the single most reliable predictor of a violent domestic relationship.*** *Unfortunately, passive partners in an abusive relationship are rarely willing to see their partners' violence for what it is. They therefore collude with the abuser in whitewashing the violence, giving the abuser tacit permission to continue the abuse.*

LOVE'S SAFETY SHATTERED

One of the most wonderful things about being in love, or having a best friend, is the feeling of safety inherent to the relationship. Our world seems so precarious much of the time. If it's not the economy, it's a natural disaster or a bomb that could go off anytime. Even a small town has its share of shootings. An intimate relationship is often the only place people feel really, truly safe and secure. Here's someone who loves you, someone who says he cares about you, someone to whom you matter more than anybody else in the world. You feel safe. Then that someone does something that shatters the safety: he uses force to emphasize a point or restrain you, he throws something at you, he threatens you. You're in shock. You don't want to believe what just happened. You don't want to admit, especially not to yourself, that the safe haven you thought you'd found from a dangerous world is a sham. Love with this person means being hurt, and whatever he calls "caring" doesn't include caring about your well-being. Suddenly the phrase "I love you to death" takes on a whole new meaning.

People don't want this to be happening; they want the fairy tale back, those wonderful three months or so at the beginning of the relationship when it all felt so magical. So they deny, discount, and explain away their partner's violence, hoping to make it all go away, never really addressing the source of the violence or dealing with it realistically.

INVENTING "REASONS" THAT MAKE THE VIOLENCE ACCEPTABLE

The Demand for Approval and Obedience

Abusers expect their partner to approve of their every word and action. It is as if there were an unspoken contract between the partners: "I (the active partner) will put you (passive partner) on a pedestal and adore you; in return you will approve of me and obey me." In the beginning of the relationship, the adoration feels so good that people are all to happy to approve of this person. They don't yet recognize the danger inherent in the "obey" part of the agreement since up until now, the passive partner pretty much agrees with all he or she has been asked to obey. "Have dinner with me," "Let me tell you how wonderful you are," "Make love with me" are all pleasant orders to obey.

Punishing the Failure to Obey

The time inevitably comes when the passive partner doesn't want to obey something the abuser has asked for, or doesn't approve of something the abuser has said or done. In healthy relationships, this is cause for discussion, exploration, and learning about the unique individual that each of us is. In abusive relationships, failure to approve of, agree with, or obey the abuser is breaking the unspoken contract. The abuser now feels entitled to punish the partner or do whatever it takes to enforce that contract.

In violent domestic relationships, the "whatever it takes" is physical force, either direct or indirect. Direct is any hands-on force: shoving, hitting, pinning you down, pulling or pushing a body part, kicking. Indirect is violence that may not directly impact you: throwing objects, tearing up the room, kicking objects, locking you in or confining you to a room or an area, walking you into a wall or other dangerous area. Both kinds of violence are usually used in combination with threats of future or further violence. This behavior is generally experienced as so devastating to the relationship that the passive partner will immediately seek to rationalize the behavior and come up with reasons to make the unacceptable acceptable in some way.

An Abuser May Be Violent
Only in the Home

"I was stunned when John walked me into the wall. I was completely unprepared for that kind of behavior from him," Mary said, "I mean, I always thought of John as a nonviolent guy." "What gave you the impression that John was nonviolent?" I asked. "Uh, nothing specific," Mary said, "just that I'd never seen him hit anybody or anything. He didn't go to bars and get into fights. He didn't talk about wanting to beat people up." "Maybe John's violence didn't come up around other people," I said, "maybe John only became violent with loved ones." "Huh," Mary said thoughtfully, "I never thought of it that way." "Abusers are not necessarily violent people per se, Mary. Much of the time the only violence they inflict is within their families. That's why all the other warning signs are so important," I said, "but let's get back to the actual event. There you are, John has walked you into the wall, what's going on with you?"

Finding Excuses

"I don't believe it," Mary said. "This can't be the man I love. I start looking for reasons. Why would he do such a thing? I don't know why I latched on to the idea of the pain pills, Dr. Noelle. I just remember that Prozac [an antidepressant] had been on the news during that time as being responsible for some people's getting violent suddenly. Some lady attacked her neighbor, I think, I don't remember exactly, but it was on the news a lot. John was taking these very powerful pain pills for his back, and I jumped on it, I thought 'That's it, that's gotta be it. It's like the Prozac, the pain pills are making John crazy.'" "You sound relieved," I said, "I was!" Mary exclaimed. "Anything was better than thinking John did that on purpose."

Accepting that your partner is responsible for the violence and that he or she deliberately and purposefully hurt you is often difficult for people. It means the end of the relationship as you knew it and the end of your safety within that relationship. Faced with two such devastating realizations, passive partners go to great lengths to excuse their partner's unacceptable violent behavior.

Karen's Hot Temper

Bob, for example, attributed Karen's violence to her hot temper. "What made it OK for Karen to express her temper physically?" I asked Bob. "I've asked myself that a lot, Doc," Bob replied. "I'm not sure. I think I put together in my mind that it was part of her being passionate. Like she was so intense and physically active in how she expressed herself sexually that it seemed only natural that she would express her anger just as intensely and as physically. At least that's what I told myself. Let's face it," Bob sighed, shaking his head, "I didn't want to look at it, I didn't want to know Karen was abusive. I mean, that's a horrible word to attach to someone, abusive. I was only too glad to excuse her on the basis of her temper."

Many people have hot tempers. Anger is a normal reaction to pain. Learning to express and channel that anger so it communicates your unhappiness or pain without damaging other people is vital to the success of a healthy loving relationship. It is one of the first skills abusers learn when they go into counseling or therapy. Getting mad or having a hot temper is not an excuse for hurting others, nor is being jealous.

It can feel wonderful to have someone be jealous of you, especially in the exciting beginnings of a relationship. How thrilling that someone should think so highly of you, value you so much, that he or she is willing to fight off anyone who tries to take you away. It's the closest most of us ever get to the passion depicted on soap operas or in romance novels. It is, however, an unfortunate approach to a real-life relationship. The way to keep someone is not to fight other people off. It is to love your partner in responsive and fulfilling ways so your partner would never want to leave.

Tony's Fear of Abandonment

Abusers live in fear of being abandoned. As much as they may mistreat you and appear indifferent to your pain, they are nonetheless extremely dependent on you. The bond they have with you is the closest experience they know to love. Anything that threatens that bond frightens abusers. When Tony told Peter how jealous he was of any flirtation or affair Peter might become involved in, Tony wasn't just being "sexy" or flattering or dramatic, he was being completely serious. He meant his threats literally. "I believed him," Peter said, "but I had no idea he would get that enraged over a situation that was history to me." "Well, the truth of it is, Peter," I said, "Tony wasn't just getting upset over the ex-lover you bumped into at the movie theater. Tony was reacting to his fear that you might abandon him. The ex-lover was just a trigger. Then, when you went to go for a walk, Tony's fear of being left, abandoned, became exacerbated. Tony's ability to cope was overwhelmed and he became violent with you." "And I was so focused on the jealousy thing," said Peter, "that I didn't see Tony's behavior as violence. I just saw it as how someone could act if you made them really jealous." "You didn't think of Tony's violence as a way Tony had of dealing with problems in general," I said. "No, absolutely not," Peter said, "the thought never occurred to me. I literally didn't get beyond thinking 'Damn, I'd better never get this guy jealous again, ever.'" "And that's where you left it?" I asked. "Unfortunately, yes," Peter said, shaking his head. "Boy was that a mistake."

Excusing Jealousy

It's a mistake all too many people make. Excusing an abuser's behavior as "Oh, he was just so jealous" is dangerous. An individual who responds with violence to jealous feelings is likely to respond to other unpleasant feelings with violence. We forget that violence is only one response to jealousy. There are other ways of dealing with such feelings that are far more beneficial, both for the success of the relationship itself and the health and well-being of both partners. Such ways include, for example, talking your feelings through with your partner, letting him know how afraid you are of his leaving, or talking your feelings through with a close friend, a counselor, or a therapist. Most people feel jealous at some time or other, but few people respond to it with violence.

You Can't Control Someone's Jealousy

Peter also made the mistake of thinking he could control Tony's violence by not provoking Tony's jealousy. Unfortunately, as too many victims of domestic violence have discovered, what provokes jealousy is in how the abuser views an event, not in the event itself, for example: A woman who buys a new perfume, for the sheer pleasure of it, finds herself accused by her husband of trying to attract other men; a man who joins a car pool to save gas is accused by his lover of joining the car pool to flirt with the other passengers; a woman who wants to go to an evening writing class is accused by her mate of finding excuses to go see her (nonexistent) lover. Abusers are astoundingly creative in the situations they can interpret as jealous provocations. No matter how hard he tried to anticipate every situation Tony might construe as jealousy-provoking, sooner or later Peter was bound to do something Tony would define as such. There is no way you can control how another individual perceives the world. It is foolhardy to think you can.

Past Violence Predicts Future Violence

Since past violence is a prime predictor of future violence, Teri should have been alerted by Anne's tales of sibling violence. Teri didn't pay attention to the warning sign. She attributed Anne's behavior to sibling rivalry, never thinking it might have something to do with how Anne generally responded to frustration, envy, and other such negative emotions. "You know, I thought it was just kid stuff," Teri said, "I didn't take it that seriously." "Ever wonder why she told you?" I asked. "No," Teri said, surprised, "I didn't." "I doubt she was doing it consciously, Teri, but Anne was letting you know how she treats those who are close to her when they get more attention that she does," I said. "People have a choice of what they are going to tell you. It's wise to ask yourself why a person would reveal that they treated someone shabbily." By excusing Anne's behavior as just sibling rivalry and kid stuff, Teri deprived herself of the very valuable information Anne had given her, information that could have warned her of the trouble ahead.

Failure to Express Remorse

"Did Anne express remorse in talking to you about what she did to her sister?" I asked. Teri laughed, "No, quite the opposite; Anne thrilled in getting away with it." "Didn't that strike you as potentially problematic?" I asked. "Anne did some pretty awful things to her sister. By the time she was an adult it would be normal to have some remorse." Nobody is perfect, and many of us have done things as children and adolescents that we're not too proud of. Most of us grow up feeling remorse over those behaviors, and we express that remorse later when we describe those experiences. Feeling badly about having done certain things is one of the things that keeps us from doing those things again. When people fail to have remorse over misdeeds, the likelihood is great that they will repeat such behavior.

YOU SAY "IT'S REALLY NOT THAT BAD"

Another way people attempt to make the violence go away is to discount it, make it appear less violent, less objectionable, less hurtful than it really is. "Well, my partner didn't hit me, so it wasn't violence" is a statement often heard from both men and women. In many instances victims of abuse discount anything short of battering. Both men and women seek to protect themselves from the awfulness of recognizing that domestic violence has just occurred by pretending it is less than it is.

"Well, at Least He Didn't Hit Me"

Mary, for example, convinced herself it wasn't that bad with the phrase "He never lifted a hand against me." That's true, John didn't, but walking someone into a wall is just as much a violent act as is hitting. Mary got hurt. Had she fallen on something sharp she could have been hurt even more. But by telling herself "He never lifted a hand against me," Mary made John's violence acceptable to her, allowing her to keep her dream relationship alive, even if it now was a little shaky.

"I used to say the same thing," Bob said, on hearing of the common response many abused individuals use to discount the violence. "I'd tell myself, Well, *it's not like she's hitting me*, she's just letting off steam and sometimes she misses and I get caught in the cross-fire." Bob laughed, "How could I have let myself believe that, Doc?! I must have been demented." "No, Bob," I said. "You were in love, and who wants to believe their lady love is a violent, abusive individual?" "Not me, that's for sure," Bob said.

The Danger of Discounting

There is a danger in discounting violence. You fool yourself into thinking things aren't as bad as they really are; consequently, you don't take a realistic look at what is going on. However, by not evaluating the situation realistically, you deny yourself the opportunity of dealing with it at this level. You allow the violence to continue, unchecked, as Peter did, for example, by discounting Tony's violence as "not so bad."

"I just wanted it to go away," Peter said, "I think I was afraid if I made a big deal about it, even just to myself, that I would have to really look at Tony differently. My beautiful love affair would be over. I didn't want that. So I made it no big deal." But by Peter making it "no big deal," oddly enough, it became a very big deal.

Violence Is Real

Teri simply passed off Anne's violence toward her sister as stories, discounting the violence by relegating it to the land of make-believe. Just as Peter and Bob failed to acknowledge the reality of their partners' violence, Teri failed to assess Anne's violence realistically, and so left herself vulnerable to the possibility of Anne abusing her. You cannot deal with something you refuse to see.

ONCE AGAIN, IT'S ALL YOUR FAULT

By rationalizing the abusive partner's violence as due to painkillers, jealousy, letting off steam, or anything else, you shift the responsibility for the violence away from the person who did it. Abusers are very willing to go along with you on that one, since, as we saw in Chapter 9, abusers refuse to accept responsibility for the negative impact of their behavior. But when it comes to violence, abusers invariably go one step further, blaming you for the violence they inflict. This causes passive partners much distress.

Making the Victim the Violator

"I'm hurt. I'm scared of what this might mean, and John is behaving like nothing happened and my bruise is my fault," Mary said. "I really did start to feel, Dr. Noelle, at about that time, that I was losing my mind. I was having trouble making sense of what was going on. All I could do was push the memory of what happened away and go on." "Did you try to talk to John about what had happened?" I asked. "No," Mary said, "I kept telling myself it was the pain pills, and maybe I should try not to contradict him while he was on those pills. He was acting so nonchalant about the whole thing. I thought I was overreacting." Mary's reaction is typical of many passive partners when abusers behave as if nothing much happened. How could anything be so wrong when your partner is behaving so normally?

Shifting Blame

Bob, in rationalizing Karen's behavior as letting off steam and just part of her hot temper, made it easy for Karen to shift all the blame to him. Convinced that Bob made her do it, Karen would then need consoling. Curiously, abusers will often turn the situation around so that they not only do the abuse, but need to be comforted for the pain you have caused them by forcing them to react violently. This truly is crazy-making. The victim ends up comforting the victimizer!

The Cycle of Domestic Violence

Much has been said and written about the cycle of domestic violence: a period of tension building, leading to a violent outburst (verbal or physical), followed by a "honeymoon" stage where the abuser is filled with remorse, apologies, and reconciliation. In none of the relationships we've been witnessing has remorse or apology been present, which may be because we have only been observing these relationships at their very beginnings.

However, even when remorse or apology is present, abusers will still usually find a way to shift responsibility for their actions onto the victim. Generally the shifting is in the guise of "If I only didn't love you so much, this wouldn't have happened," or "I can't help myself, you just make me so crazy when I see you look at someone else," followed by "I'm so sorry, it will never happen again."

Whose Hand?

Shifting responsibility allows abusers and their partners to overlook the single most critical issue: Whose hand did the hitting, shoving, throwing, or restraining? No matter how provoked you are, you are still responsible for your actions. "Tony made it very clear to me that his violence was my fault. If I hadn't made him jealous, he said, he would never have done such a thing. He was so sincere, Dr. Noelle," Peter said, "how could I not believe him? He told me loved me. He said he only 'got rough' with me, as he put it, because he loved me so much. The thought of me ever being with anyone else was too much for him to bear." "And you believed him," I said softly. "Of course I did," Peter said woefully. "What a fool I was." "No," I said, "not a fool, you just didn't want your dream to end."

Abusers often claim that love is what made them do you harm, but love is as much an action as it is a feeling. Hitting or otherwise hurting someone isn't love, it's pain. Refusal to take responsibility for causing that pain almost guarantees that abuse will happen again, and it will, once again, be the victim's fault.

SIXTEEN

How to See Violence for What It Is and Resist the Temptation to Excuse It Away

YOU INVENT REASONS TO MAKE THE VIOLENCE ACCEPTABLE TO YOU

There is a natural and very understandable tendency to want to redefine an episode of violence, past or present, to protect your image of your lover or friend as a good person. However, this is a very dangerous thing to do, as it blinds you to the reality of the relationship you are living in.

PAST VIOLENCE

Childhood and Adolescence

If your lover speaks to you of acts of violence committed in her childhood or adolescence, whether that is harm done deliberately to a sibling, a family pet, other children, grandparents, or any other individuals, listen very carefully and take the information very seriously.

Listen to whether the violence was a natural response to a provocation, such as bully picking on your friend until she finally just got fed up and socked the bully before running away as fast as she could, or whether the violence was malicious: She and her friends ganged up on a child and beat her up because this was the class nerd or other undesirable. Ask your friend how she felt about doing the violence at the time.

Listen for the presence or absence or remorse, whether your friend feels bad about having done the violence, or has regret over misdeeds. Many people have engaged in some form of violence as children and teenagers, yet have gone on to lead nonviolent lives. What distinguishes them from abusive individuals is the presence of remorse, the awareness that violence is wrong, and the regret that it happened. If your friend treats the subject lightly, as in "Oh, it was no big deal, I was just a kid," or seems to delight in the fun she had at the time, you have cause for concern. Don't invent excuses for her: If your friend experiences no remorse or regret for the damage she caused, she can readily commit such acts again.

Adulthood

If your lover speaks to you about violent acts he committed before you met, listen up! Find out as much as your can about the violence: the circumstances, the people involved, how your lover felt about it during and after, how he feels about it now. Look out for the following: Does your lover feel he was justified in using violence? Does he put the responsibility for his violent behavior on the other party? Does your lover feel that violence is an acceptable way to get things done? Does he express any remorse over the act itself or just over getting caught (if that is the case)? Restrain yourself from excusing your partner's past violence. It is wise to review this conversation with a friend or counselor to get an objective opinion of the severity of the risk to you.

Present Violence

If your lover or friend engages in any kind of violence toward you, that is, kicks you, shoves you, hits you, walks you into a wall, restrains you from leaving a room, holds you in a hurtful manner (twists your arm, grabs you), uses excessive or unwanted force during sex, throws things at you, or threatens you with any kind of violence at all, *get professional help immediately*. No excuses, no exceptions. Don't hesitate, don't wait, don't give second chances, don't think it won't happen again, don't even think it over, *get help immediately*. No matter what your lover says about the violence, no matter how sorry or indifferent or apologetic he is, *get help*. A professional will be able to tell you the alternatives available to you and counsel you appropriately according to the specifics of your situation.

Be Objective and Realistic

That being said, help yourself deal with the violence by being objective and realistic. Write down everything that happened, including what was said and done by each of you, just as it happened. Write down the actual event, what led up to the event, and what happened afterwards. As best you can, write down just the facts of what happened, not your opinion on why it happened. Don't try to explain the event away, justify it, or find good reasons why it happened, such as what *you* must have done to provoke the incident. Stick to the facts. Give that documentation to a counselor to help you understand more objectively what happened.

Write Down Your Feelings

On a separate sheet of paper, write down all your feelings about the event. Write down how you felt during the event itself, during the time leading up to it, and after. Write down how you feel now. The more truthful you are with yourself about *all* your feelings about the event, the most easily you will heal. This document will also help your counselor facilitate your healing.

Neither of these sheets of paper is for the benefit of your lover or friend. Don't leave them lying around for him to find, thinking, "Well, he really is a good person. If he only knew how much he hurt me, everything would be fine again." Maybe, but first you need to assess the situation with professional help and follow your counselor's suggestions and guidance. If your lover is not willing to take responsibility for his actions, he will only use your rendition of the facts and your statement of feelings against you. Don't take that risk.

Put the Responsibility Where It Belongs

Don't attribute your lover's violence to anything or anyone other than himself. It is not the alcohol or drugs that are responsible for your partner's violence, even though alcohol and drugs often accompany violence. It's not the pills, it's not his lousy day, it's not his rotten childhood—it's him. Don't seek to excuse your lover. Deal with the violence itself. With the help of a counselor you can discuss contributing factors as much as you like. At this point, have the courage to see the violence for what it is—inappropriate, unacceptable behavior—regardless of why it happened.

YOU DECIDE "IT'S REALLY NOT THAT BAD"

Just as it is natural to want to protect the image of the one you love by redefining the event, so too is it natural to discount the violence, pretending it was less than what it was, to protect your image of your relationship as a safe and good one. As natural as such an impulse may be, it is a foolhardy one.

Don't Dismiss the Violence

Your lover is often only too willing to help you view the violence as less than what it really was. Don't buy into his dismissal of the violence: "Oh, it was just a love tap, what are you crying about?" "I missed, didn't I? What's the big deal?" "It's not as if I mean to hurt you, I just wanted to make my point!"

Get Help

Do not trust yourself to view the violence with any degree of objectivity. You are emotionally shaken and probably not thinking straight. The facts of the event that you wrote down will help a counselor assess the violence more realistically than you can. The counselor can then work with you on your understanding and acceptance of the violence for what it is.

Be Honest about What Happened

Don't pretend it won't happen again. In all probability, it will. Don't delude yourself into thinking it wasn't as bad as it was: "Well, at least he didn't hit me." "It's just a bruise, it's not that big a deal." "Well, he just threatened me, he wouldn't really do anything." Any violence is bad. Any violence is a breach of the tacit agreement that allows us to feel secure and function safely within our relationships. Fear makes a lousy bed partner.

ONCE AGAIN, IT'S ALL YOUR FAULT

Abusers refuse to take responsibility for their violence. Somehow, they will twist and turn events so that the violence they inflicted on you becomes your fault: "Well you're just so clumsy, if you'd look where you're going you wouldn't run into things." "If you didn't get me so mad, I wouldn't hit you." "If you didn't make me jealous, I'd never get rough with you, you know it's only because I love you so much." "If you didn't get me so frustrated, I'd never throw stuff." "You've been at me all day, just asking for it." "You think I feel good about what I did?" "Of course I don't, but I can't help it, you made me do it."

Abusers Want Consoling

Because abusers see their violence as your fault, often they need consoling: "I feel so bad about what I did, I love you so much," they cry, as if that justified everything, expecting you to wipe off their tears. All too often, that's exactly what passive partners do. It's almost unbearable to believe that someone who is so close to you, who swears he loves you, could possibly do you such harm. Victim and victimizer collude in the myth of "It's a one-time thing, it will never happen again, I didn't mean to do it, I love you so."

The Eloquent Apology

Abusers are often eloquent in their apology and re-morse after the fact. They may treat you wonderfully for a while, apologizing constantly, and trying to make up and bring the magic back into the relationship. Stay strong! No matter what they say, they have violated the implicit contract of safety and security fundamental to a loving relationship. Even if his apology is completely genuine, your partner needs help dealing with his violent be-havior.

Hitting Never Means Love

Love is not about hitting people. Don't join in the collusion. Keep your sense of reality, stay grounded. Ask yourself: "Whose hand hit me?" "Whose hand threw something at me?" "Whose hand shoved me?" "Whose foot kicked me?" "Whose mouth threatened me?" Who-ever's hand, foot, mouth, or other body part hurt you is the individual responsible for the violence, no one else. Certainly not you, no matter how hard your lover or friend tries to convince you of such. Your contribution to the violence was your unwillingness, as the relationship unfolded, to see and deal with the reality of all the other kinds of abuse—the blaming, the criticizing, the posses-sive behavior that preceded the violence. The responsibil-ity you have now is to get help and heal yourself.

Take Action Immediately

Don't wait to get help, thinking the abuser will see the error of his ways over time. That's highly unlikely. The stronger likelihood is that after a brief period of calm, your lover will feel the buildup of internal pressure, which will once again erupt in violence toward you. *Once an incident of domestic violence has occurred, that violence will escalate with each episode; the battering is progressive and usually will not stop until one of the partners dies.* Don't wait for the next violent episode. Take care of yourself. If you have been involved in one instance of domestic violence, you are at risk of more.

"Does this mean," you ask, "that if there is one incident of violence in a relationship, the relationship is over? That the only sane thing to do is leave?" No, it's not that simple. The only sane thing to do is to get help and, with the help of a professional, determine the best course of action. If your lover is willing to get help, understands how he is responsible for his actions, and learns new ways of dealing with stress and frustration, the relationship can survive. But you can't do it alone. It may be lethal to try.

Mary, Bob, Peter, and Teri Revisited

SEVENTEEN

New Beginnings

MARY'S SESSION

It had been over a year since I last saw Mary. She looked well, more relaxed than when I had worked with her previously. Her visit today was the one-year follow-up we had agreed on. I was looking forward to finding out how she was doing.

Mary looked around the office, "The place hasn't changed much," she said. "No, it stays pretty much the same," I said, smiling. Mary sat down. "How have you been?" I asked. "Well," Mary replied, "very well, actually. I'm in a relationship now, and I think it's OK, Dr. Noelle. I really think it's OK." "You sound a little dubious about it," I said. Mary laughed, "I'm hypercautious, that's all." "Want to tell me about it?" I asked. "I'd like that, " Mary said. "Actually, what I'd like to tell you about is how differently this relationship came together." "All right," I said, ready to listen.

Mary settled herself on the couch, then began her story: "After I completed my therapy with you, I didn't date at all for about three months. I needed some time alone, some time to just—be. And that felt good. And after that, I started accepting blind dates and letting myself be open to the idea of a relationship. I met some nice men, but nothing really happened, no 'sparks.' Until Gus came along." Mary shook her head. "I knew I was in trouble then. Here was this nice-looking man who really was attracted to me, and I was very attracted to him. You'd think I'd be happy about it, but I was scared to death, Dr. Noelle. It started just like with John, the attention, all the romance, the works. I got really, really scared. But I didn't want to just walk away. So I decided that it was OK to be scared, and I could do this. I could pay enough attention to what was going on so that I'd know if this relationship was going to be like the one with John and turn out ugly, or if it was going to be different." Mary paused for a moment. "You had a lot of courage, Mary," I said. "It is scary to open up to trusting someone again, no matter how much healing has happened."

Mary nodded, then went on: "I thought back to all the stuff we had worked on, and I took it real slow. I figured if I just take things slow enough, I'll see what's going on. I won't get 'drugged' by all the romance like I did with John. So that's what I did. Gus wanted to see me all the time. I said, 'No, I don't think that's a good idea,' and for the first month, I would only see him on weekends. I know that sounds really structured, but it's the only way I could keep myself from seeing him all the time." Mary laughed. "I thought of it as my 'Gus diet,' you know, like when you only get to eat ice cream on the weekend 'cause you're trying to lose weight." Mary got serious once again, "But it did work, Dr. Noelle. I stood my ground and although Gus didn't understand at the beginning and squawked a bit, he went along with it.

What surprised me is how much better I felt about how the relationship was developing. I didn't feel off center and kind of 'high' all the time. I don't know how to explain this very well, but it felt more 'real,' more solid somehow. Then, when we started seeing each other a little more, a night or two in the week, it felt OK; I felt like we were both interested in getting to know the other."

"Like it was more about the people involved and less about the emotions of meeting each other?" I asked, "Yes, that's a good way of putting it," Mary said, reflecting, "and part of that had to do with the fact that we weren't sleeping together yet. Since we weren't using sex as a way to get to know each other, we had to talk. And that really worked for me."

"Was your not having sex a conscious choice, Mary, or something that just happened?" I asked, curious. "Oh, it was very conscious," Mary replied. "I figured that one of the things that got me in trouble with John was my sleeping with him early on. I know myself. When I sleep with somebody I tend to get real attached, so if I slept with Gus before I had really had a chance to see who he was, I was afraid I'd be making myself vulnerable to another bad relationship." I nodded: I was very familiar with Mary's experience of sleeping with someone and getting immediately attached, having heard it from many women clients and some men.

"When I finally did sleep with Gus, it really was wonderful, Dr. Noelle, because by then we knew each other quite a bit. I was really comfortable with him and felt trusting of him, and we already cared for each other a lot. So the sex added to a relationship that was already good, making it that much better. Before, with John, I felt like the sex somehow made the relationship, that it was because of the sex that we cared." Mary sighed, then continued: "Another thing I liked about Gus was that even though he pursued me real hard, whenever I asked him to slow down, he would. I might have to ask a couple of times, but it did work. What's funny is I was so determined now to get into another abusive relationship that I was willing to lose Gus rather than give in to something that didn't feel right to me. And I think that's what made it possible for me to set my limits.

"I did another thing that was new for me, Dr. Noelle," Mary said, "I didn't give up my life." "I beg your pardon?" I asked, not understanding. "I didn't stop all the other parts of my life," Mary replied, "I kept seeing my friends as often as usual, kept going to the gym, didn't drop my hobbies, but I'll tell you, it was hard!" I smiled, "I can well understand that, Mary, a new love is compelling." "We've been seeing each other about six months now," Mary said, "and last week Gus told me he really respected that about me, that I had a life and I didn't drop it all just to be with him all the time." She grinned, "My friends were happier about it too. I found out they were none too pleased when I ignored all of them the whole time I was with John."

"Anyway," Mary continued, "we still aren't living together. I'm too scared. And Gus seems to be OK with our taking time. The 'hot romance' part has calmed down; I don't feel like he's 'on the make' all the time. It feels like a real friendship is developing between us. It feels good." "It sounds good, Mary," I said, "you are on the right track."

Thoughts on Mary's Session

Mary's way of ensuring that she didn't allow an abusive relationship to develop was to treat herself with respect. She acted in accordance with a time framework that felt right for her to see Gus and eventually have sex with him. She didn't give up her friendships or her activities for the sake of this new relationship. She wasn't planning to move in with Gus until she became truly comfortable with the idea.

All of these choices reflect Mary's valuing of herself and her life. She behaved in a way that made her inaccessible to an abusive individual. An abusive individual would not have been able to wait for Mary to come to levels of comfort and trust that felt right to her. An abusive individual would not have accepted Mary's seeing her friends and continuing her lifestyle as she preferred. He would have been long gone.

Is there still a possibility that Mary's new relationship will end up in violence? All things are possible, but that possibility decreases significantly with each situation in which Mary values herself and Gus respects Mary's choices. Given how the relationship is progressing, violence is highly unlikely.

BOB'S LETTER

"Dear Dr. Noelle," Bob's letter began, "I'm sorry I couldn't make our follow-up session in person, but when my ex-wife moved up north, I moved there also in order to be closer to my kids. I'm hardly ever in town anymore. So I hope this letter fills you in sufficiently on what's been going on; if you want to know more, just give me a call.

"I'm alive and well, but not kicking very much. Things have been pretty quiet in my emotional life since I last saw you. I can't believe it's been a year already—time does fly! I've tried to date, off and on, but I just can't seem to get that part of my life going again. Part of it is I'm scared, but think if I met someone really exciting, I could get past the fears. I do feel I learned enough in our session time together to know the danger signs, and enough about myself to know how I can let emotions get the better of me and what to do about it. No, the weird thing is, I really like being alone.

"Maybe I'm fooling myself, but there's a lot to be said for the peace and quiet of my life right now. I never appreciated it before. Maybe because I used to feel pretty lonely when I was alone. I don't feel that way much any more. I've been devoting a lot more time to my kids. I felt so bad about not being there for them the whole time I was involved with Karen, I missed an important part of their growing-up years. So I've been making up for it, I guess. I see the kids a lot, and their mother is pleased about that. It gets them out of her hair for a while so she can spend some time with her boyfriend, and I love it.

"I help the kids with school projects, go to baseball games and stuff like that with them. I even go to PTA meetings! That's been a nice social thing for me, Dr. Noelle, PTA and all the parents, single or otherwise, that I've been meeting through spending so much time with the kids. Maybe that's why I'm not as lonely as I thought I'd be. I have a lot of friends and people I can do things with pretty much any time. And I pay as much attention to making sure the friends in my life aren't the abusive kind as I would if I were out there courting, believe me. I took to heart your saying that domestic violence isn't about love, it's about relationship. I'm well aware now that abuse can happen in any relationship, friends or lovers, so I set limits with people and make sure I only get involved with people that seem to be unselfish and caring, people who have a lot of space in their heart for others.

"Do I miss not having someone special in my life? Not really, but I miss Karen. It sounds so strange to say this, Dr. Noelle, and I don't think I could say it to anybody else but you, but I do miss her. Oh, I don't miss the throwing and the yelling and all that, heck no, but I do miss the good parts—the passion, the excitement, and the fun! Gosh, I had more fun with Karen in that short couple of months right at the beginning when it was good than I ever had with anybody in my whole life. I wouldn't do it again, for anything—the pain just hurt too much, but I surely would like to find some of that passion and excitement again, somehow.

"In the meantime, I do a lot of 'good Dad' things and enjoy my life, taking it one day at a time. Maybe someday I'll find a lady with the passion and the fun—who doesn't throw things. I'm certainly going to keep looking.

Hoping this letter finds you well,"

Bob

Comments on Bob's Letter

Bob's reaction is not unusual. Many people, having survived a violent domestic relationship, find solace in peace and quiet. Attending to his family and rebuilding his relationship with his children facilitates his own healing, as does creating new friendships.

Bob's missing Karen is also not unusual. Abusive individuals, for all their downsides, are often captivating, exciting, wonderfully dramatic individuals who generate enormous passion and excitement. If you have little excitement, drama, and passion in your life, such individuals may be extremely attractive to you and once they are gone, you may feel cruelly the lack of intensity. The best antidote to such a lack is to fill it for yourself. Rather than waiting for another individual to come along and provide you with excitement and passion, search actively for ways to generate those feelings for yourself. Hobbies and interests often provide great ways of doing so: People can get passionate about everything from participating in volunteer programs to sports to learning to paint or joining the community theater group.

If you are providing intensity and excitement for yourself, you won't be so lacking that you are irresistibly pulled to the next passionate person you meet regardless of his or her potential for violence. You will be in a much better position to see the person for who he or she is, warts and all, and to figure out if this is someone with whom you can have a healthy relationship.

PETER'S VISIT

Peter came in smiling to our follow-up appointment. He gave me a big hug before he sat down on the couch. He looked fit and healthy, a few pounds lighter than when I'd last seen him a little under a year ago. "It's good to see you," he said, "it's been a while." "Thanks, Peter," I said, "it's good to see you, too. So you want to know how things have been going, right?" Peter asked, getting right down to business. "Yes, I do," I said, "very much so."

"OK," Peter said, and he was off and running: "Things have been good, especially lately. For about the first six months after our last session, I pretty much kept to myself. I did a lot of thinking about everything that went on, did a lot of thinking about my life in general, and made some changes."

"Like what?" I asked. "Well, to start, I decided to go back to school so I could do something different with my life. It suddenly dawned on me I wasn't going to be young and cute forever," Peter grinned. I said nothing, just smiled, "OK, young forever," Peter said, laughing. "Anyway, I've been taking these computer classes. I figured if I knew how to work a computer I could probably get a better job almost anywhere. So I'm going to these classes after work and on Saturdays, and I'm meeting a lot of people there. Not men to date," Peter hastened to add, "I was in no way ready to date. I mean people: men, women, young, old, staight, gay—whatever. So I thought, well, heck, I might as well try to practice some of that stuff I learned at Dr. Noelle's about people so that by the time I am ready to start dating again maybe I'll be better able to spot abusive type men and not get involved with them. And that's what I did. I practiced. And what I found out, much to my surprise, is how much people tell you about who they really are if you know how to listen for it."

"What do you mean, Peter?" I asked. "Well," Peter said, "for example, there was this one older guy who had a lot of trouble with learning the computer: He was in his fifties maybe, having to retrain because he'd lost the job he'd had forever with this company. He was real bitter about it. Anyway, every time the teacher would point out something he was doing wrong, this guy would blame it on something or someone else. He'd say someone jogged his elbow and that's why he made a mistake, or the keyboard was a lousy piece of equipment, or the teacher wasn't a good communicator. It was absolutely amazing! That man couldn't take responsibility for anything.

"Before I'd started coming to you, Dr. Noelle, I never would have paid any attention to that kind of thing, I'd have thought, 'Oh, poor guy, he's just having a rough time.' I would have just passed it off as meaningless. So I kept listening to this guy to see what else I could find out, and I realized he was real critical of other people. If someone passed one of the computer tests really well, he'd say the person must have brown-nosed their way into the grade, or gotten extra tutoring from the teacher by kissing up. If someone did poorly, he'd practically gloat. This guy was a trip! But what amazed me most, Dr. Noelle, was how little I actually listened to people before. What I mean is, I heard the words, but I didn't know what the deeper meaning was behind the words. I didn't know how much words reveal of what is going on with someone." I nodded, "Words aren't just something to fill up the silence or report on an activity, words are just what you say they are Peter, they reveal what is going on with someone. It's great that you were able to experience that as fully as you did."

"Well, it sure made a difference when I started dating again," Peter said. "Boy did I listen. And I watched. I watched how guys would treat bartenders and waiters and cashiers and everyone else around when we were out together. I watched to see if they treated me nice to get me going but were indifferent to everybody else. I paid attention when a guy started saying stuff that seemed too good to be true. And I started talking." "Talking?" I asked, intrigued. "Uh-huh," Peter said, "if someone said something to me I thought was over the top, like 'You're the greatest guy I've ever met,' I'd say 'Tell me more about that, in what way am I the greatest guy, what does that mean to you at this point in your life?' I mean, I wasn't digging for flattery, I wanted to see what was really behind the words."

I laughed in appreciation, "That's great, Peter! What a different approach to courtship." "Yup," Peter said, "sure stops people in their tracks—or should I say in their b.s. And I did that with pretty much everything I saw or heard that didn't seem right, stuff that reminded me of what Tony would say and do. So, for example, if a guy was late for a date and started implying it was my fault 'cause I had suggested the time we meet, I'd ask him to tell me more about that, and I'd start digging to see how much this guy was into blame. Sometimes dates ended real quickly that way," Peter said, smiling, "and that was fine by me. I don't need to spend so much as another week involved with an abusive guy. I had enough of that with Tony to last me a lifetime." "I hear you on that one," I said.

"Then I met Mark," Peter continued, "and all that practice paid off. Because what I found out, Dr. Noelle, is someone doesn't have to be perfect, they can have their own little criticalness or blaming behavior or over the top stuff, but, if you can talk about it, it's OK. You can work it out. And Mark calls me on my stuff, too. When I pass things off as not important, or I don't stand up for myself enough in situations, he calls me on it. It's good, Dr. Noelle, it feels like a relationship, where both of us are trying to make things good for the other and for each of us." "That's great, Peter," I said, "I am really happy for you, for both of you." "Thanks," Peter said, "I owe you a lot." "No, you don't, Peter," I said, "I gave you the skills, yes, but you're the one who had the courage to go out in the world and actually use those skills in a way that worked for you. That's terrific."

"Well, Mark hasn't moved in yet, nor have I moved into his place," Peter said. "We're both taking it slow, mostly because I insist on it. And I'm taking it day by day, Dr. Noelle, day by day." "The best way to go, Peter," I said, "and the surest way to get where you want to go."

Reflections on Peter's Visit

The skills I taught Peter, the skills outlined in this book, are only as valuable as your willingness to put them into practice in your life. Peter's discovering for himself that people really do reveal themselves in how they talk is worth more than a thousand lectures on the subject. If you are willing to listen deeply to what people say, ask yourself and them about the significance of what they say, think about the answers they give you, you will discover who truly lives inside that person, and be able to differentiate between abusive and nonabusive individuals with surprising ease. Watching people as they interact with others and the environment around them is also extremely valuable. People most often reveal their true selves when they believe they are unobserved.

You don't have to spend your life being scared of getting involved with a damaging human being. You can use your wonderful human gifts of observation and thought to sort out those who will bring joy to your life and those who will bring pain.

TERI SENDS AN E-MAIL

"Dear Dr. Noelle," begins the letter from Teri, "I'll bet you're surprised to hear from me on your e-mail!" That I was. I was fully expecting to see Teri sometime in the next couple of weeks. "I've been transferred to an 'in the field' position, and I'm all over the country every day. I didn't know when I'd be able to get in for our follow-up session, so I thought I'd fill you in this way." I printed out Teri's letter and sat down to read it.

"I've been busy since the last session I had with you. Work has been great, I've really been enjoying this company. I guess if I had to sum up what's different for me now, it's that I feel much more confident about who I am and the choices I make for myself. I've realized that one of the reasons I was so susceptible to Anne was that I didn't think much of my ability to make good choices for myself. I've found out I can do that pretty well. I listen to people's opinion about things, but I don't do what people suggest just because they have suggested it any more. I think about it, I look into things more for myself, sit with myself and think about things more, and that seems to be working out just fine. I've found out I like living according to 'Teri's Way,' even if it's not how other people live. That's not as selfish as it might sound. I like to do for other people and help out and things like that, I'm just not real keen on someone telling me 'Well you should …' or 'You know you'd make a great … ' and going for it without an awful lot of my own thought going in to the decision.

"I don't have a roommate, I just couldn't do that yet. One day I'm sure I'll be able to, but I still wake up in the night every so often, scared to death for no apparent reason. I don't want to always live alone, but it's OK for now; I figure I have plenty of time in front of me still. I found a tiny studio apartment I just love that I share with two cats and lots of plants.

"And yes, I am dating, but only on a friend basis at this point. The thing with Anne made me realize just how naive I was in my approach to letting someone in my life. I took people too much at face value, not that there aren't plenty of good people who do say what they mean and mean what they say, only that I need to get better at sorting out the frogs from the princes. I don't want to make the same mistakes with a romance. I've learned I'm a valuable human being and I'm not willing to get involved with a man who doesn't see and respect that value. I have a lot more to learn about people before I'm willing to give my heart away.

That's about it for now, I guess. I'll check in again next year—or sooner if anything major happens. Thanks again for all your help,"

Teri

Lessons Learned

It takes time to recover from domestic violence, and Teri is wise to take the time she needs to heal. We are all valuable human beings, no matter how imperfect. Your willingness to respect your own value goes a long way toward ensuring that the other close persons in your life respect it also.

Although Teri's experience with domestic violence had nothing to do with a romantic involvement, she is using what she learned from the relationship with Anne to build a healthy love relationship for herself in the future, one based on an increased awareness of how people behave and on respect for herself and others.

Conclusion

You don't have to be another statistic of domestic violence. If you see any of the warning signs described in this book, pay attention! Most potentially violent people will display some, if not all, of these signs. Don't be fooled. Such people often start off as a nice guy or gal. Use your common sense and your own gut feelings to guide you.

Always take the time to get to know a person. Give yourself the opportunity to see how the person behaves in many different situations before you give your heart away. And don't give your heart away all at once. Give pieces of your heart, slowly, as you come to discover if the person is indeed what they seem. Over time, people will inevitably show their true colors. You are a valuable human being. Your well-being is worth your taking that time.

Trust how you feel in the relationship. Do you feel happy, safe, secure? Or are you a little anxious, too eager to please, afraid of doing the "wrong thing"? Do you feel valued, listened to, your thoughts and feelings being taken very much into account? Or do you feel the attention always seems to revolve around the other person, that you have to say things over and over and still do not feel heard, that your emotions don't seem to matter, do not count? Pay attention to these feelings, they are meaningful. Your feelings are your own internal warning system, letting you know if you are in a relationship that is good and healthy for you or not.

Observe how people treat others and the world around them, their family, their friends, their co-workers, the people they get services from, everyone they interact with. This will tell you a great deal about the kind of individuals they really are. People tend to be consistent with themselves. People who have little regard for the well-being of others, who have little respect for the community they live in, the world they inhabit, the environment that supports their existence, will have little regard for you. As special as these individuals make you feel in the beginning, they will eventually come to treat you just as they treat all others in their world— with one difference—they will treat you worse.

Don't become another victim of domestic violence. When you see these warning signs, be smart, walk away. Go find real love—the kind that doesn't hurt.

Recommended Readings

Harriet B. Braiker, *Lethal Lovers and Poisonous People: How to Protect Your Health from Relationships that Make You Sick*, Pocket Star Books, New York, 1992.

Jerry Brinegar, *Breaking Free from Domestic Violence*, Compcare Publishers, Minneapolis, Minnesota, 1992.

Connell Cowen and Melvyn Kinder, *Smart Women, Foolish Choices: Finding the Right Men and Avoiding the Wrong Ones*, Crown, New York, 1985.

Barbara DeAngelis, *Are You the One for Me? Knowing Who's Right and Avoiding Who's Wrong*, Dell, New York, 1992.

Beverly Engel, *The Emotionally Abused Woman*, Fawcett Columbine Books, New York, 1990.

Susan Forward, *Men Who Hate Women and the Women Who Love Them*, Bantam Books, New York, 1986.

Ann Jones, *Next Time She'll Be Dead*, Beacon, Boston, 1994.

Barry Levy, *In Love and in Danger: A Teen Guide to Breaking Free of Abusive Relationships*, Seal Press, Seattle, Washington, 1992.

Dangerous Relationships

Kerry Lobel, ed., *Naming the Violence: Speaking Out about Lesbian Battering: Anthology*, Seal Press, Seattle, Washington, 1986.

Ann Rule, *Dead by Sunset: Perfect Husband, Perfect Killer?*, Pocket Books, New York, 1996.

Resources

The following is a list of national organizations that can assist you with information, help, and recovery from domestic violence.

National Domestic Violence Hotline
1-800-799-7233
For the hearing impaired: 1-800-787-3224

National Organization for Victim Assistance Hotline
1-800-870-6682

Battered Women's Justice Project
%National Clearinghouse for the Defense of Battered Women
125 South 9th Street, Suite 302
Philadelphia, PA 19107
215-351-0010

Center for the Prevention of Sexual and Domestic Violence
936 North 34th Street, Suite 200
Seattle, WA 98103
206-634-1903

Family Violence Prevention Fund
383 Rhode Island Street, Suite 304
San Francisco, CA 94103-5133
415-252-8900

National Coalition against Domestic Violence
Policy Office
P.O. Box 34103
Washington, DC 20043-4103
703-765-0339

National Network to End Domestic Violence
Policy Office
701 Pennsylvania Avenue N.W., Suite 900
Washington, DC 20004
202-434-7405

National Resource Center on Domestic Violence
Pennsylvania Coalition against Domestic Violence
6400 Flank Drive, Suite 1300
Harrisburg, PA 19107
800-537-2238

Texas Council on Family Violence
8701 North Mopac Expressway, Suite 450
Austin, TX 78759
512-794-1133

Personalized Safety Plan

The following steps represent my plan for increasing my safety and preparing in advance for the possibility of further violence. Although I do not have control over my partner's violence, I do have a choice about *how* to respond to him/her and how to best get myself and my children to safety.

Step 1: Safety during a violent incident. Women cannot always avoid violent incidents. In order to increase safety, battered women may use a variety of strategies.

From the Texas Council on Family Violence, 8701 North Mopac Expressway, Suite 450, Austin, TX 78759, January, 1995. Adapted from Barbara Hart and Jane Stuehling, Pennsylvania Coalition Against Domestic Violence, 6400 Flank Drive, Suite 1300, Harrisburg, PA 17112, PCADV, 1992. Adapted from Personalized Safety Plan, Office of the City Attorney, City of San Diego, California, April 1990. Reprinted with permission from: Pennsylvania Coalition Against Domestic Violence, 6400 Flank Drive, Suite 1300, Harrisburg, PA 17112.

I can use some or all of the following strategies:

A. If I decide to leave, I will _____ .
   (Practice how to get out safely. What doors, windows, elevators, stairwells, or fire escapes would I use?)

B. I can keep my purse and car keys ready and put them _____ (place) in order to leave quickly.

C. I can tell _____ about the violence and request s/he call the police if s/he hears suspicious noises coming from my house.

D. I can teach my children how to use the telephone to contact the police and the fire department. (Be careful about placing responsibility on children.)

E. I will use _____ as my code word with my children or my friends so they can call for help.

F. If I have to leave my home, I will go _____.
   (Decide this even if I don't think there will be a next time.) If I cannot go to this location above, then I can go to _____ or _____ .

G. I can also teach some of these strategies to some/all of my children.

H. When I expect we are going to have an argument, I will try to move to a space that is lowest risk, such as

   _____ .

   (Try to avoid arguments in the bathroom, garage, kitchens, near weapons, or in rooms without access to an outside door.)

I. I will use my judgment and intuition. If the situation is very serious, I can give my partner what s/he wants to calm him/her down. I have to protect myself until I/we are out of danger.

Step 2: Safety when preparing to leave. Battered women frequently leave the residence they share with the battering partner. Leaving must be done with a careful plan in order to increase safety. Batterers often strike back when they believe that a battered woman is leaving a relationship.

I can use some or all of the following safety strategies:

A. I will leave money and an extra set of keys with _____ so I can leave quickly.

B. I will keep copies of important documents (see Step 8) or keys at _____ .

C. I will open an individual savings account by _____ (date) to increase my independence or I will find a safe place to hide cash.

D. Other things I can do to increase my independence include: _____
_____
_____
_____
_____

E. The domestic violence program's hotline number is
_____ .
I can seek shelter by calling this hotline. I will call ahead of time to find out the procedure for admission to the shelter.

F. I can keep change for phone calls on me at all times. I understand that if I use my telephone credit card, the following month the telephone bill will tell my batterer those numbers that I called after I left. To keep my telephone communications confidential, I must either use coins or I might get a friend to permit me to use their telephone credit card for a limited time when I first leave.

G. I will check with _____ and _____ to see who would be able to let me stay with them or lend me some money.

H. I can leave extra clothes with _____ .

I. I will sit down and review my safety plan every _____ (no less than 6 weeks) in order to plan the safest way to leave the residence. _____ (domestic violence advocate or friend) has agreed to help me review this plan.

J.   I will rehearse my escape plan and, as appropriate, practice it with my children.

Step 3: Safety in my own residence. (If my partner leaves or is forced to leave or I am in a new home.) There are many things that a woman can do to increase her safety in her own residence. It may be impossible to do everything at once, but safety measures can be added step by step. *Never assume my partner won't find me!*

Safety measures I can use include:

A.   I can change the locks on my doors and windows as soon as possible.

B.   I can replace wooden doors with steel/metal doors.

C.   I can install security systems including additional locks, keyless deadbolts, window bars (not generally recommended because of fire escape hazards), poles to wedge against doors, an electronic alarm system, etc.

D.   I can purchase rope ladders ("fire ladders" are available from hardware and discount stores) to be used for escape from second-floor windows.

E.   I can install smoke detectors and purchase fire extinguishers for each floor in my house/apartment.

F.   I can install an outside lighting system (motion detectors) that lights up when a person is coming close to my house.

G.   I will teach my children how to use the telephone to make a collect call to me and to _____ (friend/minister/other) in the event that my partner takes the children.

H.   I will tell people who take care of my children which people have permission to pick up my children and that my partner is not permitted to do so. Some will require a court order. The people I will inform about pick-up permission include:

_____ (school),

_____ (daycare staff),

_____ (babysitter),

_____ (Sunday school teacher),

_____ (teacher), and

_____ (others).

I. I can inform _____ (neighbor), _____ (pastor), and _____ (friend) that my partner no longer resides with me and they should call the police if s/he is observed near my residence.

Step 4: Safety with a protective order. Many batterers obey protective orders, but one can never be sure which violent partner will obey and which will violate protective orders. I recognize that I may need to ask the police and the courts to enforce my protective order.

The following are some steps that I can take to help with the enforcement of my protective order:

A. I will keep a *certified copy* of my protective order (and/or probation orders or other such legal documents) _____ (location). (Always keep it on or near my person. If I change purses, that's the first thing that should go in.)

B. The District Clerk should contact all law enforcement agencies in my area. I will make sure my protective order is filed properly with the District Clerk by calling _____.

C. I will verify that my protective order has been sent to police/sheriff's departments in the community where I work, in those communities where I usually visit family or friends, and in the community where I live by calling _____ (law enforcement agency). I may need to include my family/friends in my protective order.

D. If my partner destroys my protective order, I can get another certified copy from the courthouse by going to the District Clerk located at _____. The fee for this is $____.

E. For further safety, if I often visit other counties, I might file my protective order with the law enforcement agencies in those counties. I will register my protective order in the following counties: _____, _____ and _____. (If I move to another county, I will modify my protective order. Again, I will check with local law enforcement agencies.)

F. I can call my domestic violence advocate if I am not sure about B, C, D, or E or if I have some problem with my protective order. The number to call is _____.

G. I will inform my employer, my minister, my closest friend, and _____ and _____ that I have a protective order in effect (maybe give them copies, too).

H. If my partner violates the protective order, I can call the police and report a violation, contact my attorney, call my advocate, and/or advise the court of the violation. (*I will make sure it gets documented!*)

I. If the police do not help, I can contact my advocate or attorney and/or file a complaint with the chief of the police department. My attorney's name is _____, and his/her phone number is _____.

Step 5: Safety on the job and in public. Each battered woman must decide if and when she will tell others that her partner has battered her and that she may be at continued risk. Friends, family and coworkers can help to protect women. Each woman should consider carefully which people to invite to help secure her safety.

I might do any or all of the following:

A. I can inform my supervisor, the security supervisor, and _____ at work of my situation.
B. I can ask _____ to help screen my telephone calls at work.
C. When leaving work, I can _____
   _____.
D. When driving home, if problems occur, I can _____
   _____.
E. If I use public transit, I can _____
   _____.
F. I can use different grocery stores and shopping malls to conduct my business and shop at hours that are different to those I used when residing with my battering partner.
G. I can use a different bank and take care of my banking at hours different from those I used when residing with my battering partner.
H. I can also _____.
I. I will always remember to be careful and watchful. I must always "look over my shoulder" and be cautious of any person or car that might be following me.

Step 6: Safety and drug or alcohol use. Most people in this culture use alcohol. Many use mood-altering drugs. Much of this use is legal, and some is not. The legal outcomes of using illegal drugs can be very hard on a battered woman and may hurt her relationship with her children and put her at a disadvantage in other legal actions with her battering partner. Women should carefully consider the potential cost of the use of illegal drugs. *The use of alcohol or other drugs can reduce a woman's awareness and ability to act quickly to protect herself from her battering partner.* The use of alcohol or other drugs by the batterer may give him/her an excuse to use violence.

If drug or alcohol use has occurred in my relationship with the battering partner, I can enhance my safety by some or all of the following:

A. If I am going to use, I can do so in a safe place and with people who understand the risk of violence and are committed to my safety.
B. I can also _____.
C. If my partner is using, I can _____.
D. I might also _____.
E. To safeguard my children, I might _____ and _____.

Step 7: Safety and my emotional health. The experience of being battered and verbally degraded by one's partner is usually exhausting and emotionally draining. The process of building a new life for myself takes *much courage and incredible energy.*

To conserve my emotional energy and resources and to avoid hard emotional times, I can do some of the following:

A. If I feel down and ready to return to a potentially abusive situation, I can _____.
B. When I have to communicate with my partner in person or by telephone, I can _____.
C. I can try to use "I can ... " statements with myself and to be assertive with others.
D. I can tell myself "_____" whenever I feel others are trying to control or abuse me.
E. I can read _____ to help me feel stronger.
F. I can call _____, _____, and _____ as other resources to be of support to me.
G. Other things I can do to help me feel stronger are _____, _____, and _____.

H.   I can take care of myself by _____
     '_____ , and _____ .
I.   I can attend workshops and support groups at the
     domestic violence program or _____ ,
     _____ , or _____ to gain support and
     strengthen my relationships with other people.

Step 8: Items to take when leaving. When women leave
partners, it is important to take certain items with them.
Women sometimes give an extra copy of papers and an
extra set of clothing to a friend just in case they have to
leave quickly.

Items with check marks on the following list are the most
important to take. If there is time, the other items might be
taken or stored outside the home. These items might best
be placed in one location, so that if we have to leave in a
hurry, I can grab them quickly.

When I leave, I should take:

✓   Identification for myself
✓   My birth certificate
✓   Children's birth certificates
✓   Social Security cards
✓   School and vaccination records
✓   Driver's license and registration
✓   Money
✓   Checkbook, ATM card
✓   Credit cards
✓   Keys: house, car, office
✓   Medications
✓   Work permits
✓   Green card
✓   Welfare identification
    Lease/rental agreement, house deed, mortgage pay-
    ment book

Financial documents (i.e., income tax records, savings accounts, bank books, IRAs)
Children's favorite toys and/or blankets
Items of special sentimental value
Car title(s)
Marriage/divorce certificates
Passport(s)
Medical records (for all family members)
Insurance papers
Address book
Small saleable objects
Jewelry
Pictures

Telephone numbers I need to know:

Police Department—home _____
Police Department—school _____
Police Department—work _____
Domestic Violence Hotline _____
Domestic Violence Advocate _____
District Clerk (for registry of protective orders) ___
Work number _____
Supervisor's home number _____
Minister _____
Attorney _____
School/daycare _____
Doctor _____
Friend _____
Family member _____
Other _____

Index

Dangerous Relationships

Dangerous Relationships